Christianity in Today's China

Taking Root Downward, Bearing Fruit Upward

Christianity in Today's China

Taking Root Downward,
Bearing Fruit Upward

by

Britt Towery

Foreword by David M. Paton

The Tao Foundation Missionary
Heritage Edition
A.D. 2000

1stBooks - rev. 10/11/00

Books by Britt Towery

EVERYONE PREACHING CHRIST, by Princeton S. Hsu (translated).1968

A BIBLE OUTLINE: The New Testament
(co-author with Peter Tong). 1975

PATTERNS
(co-author with Jody Towery). 1986

THE PENGLAI-PINGDU BAPTIST MEMORIALS
Stories of Southern Baptist pioneers in Shandong China. 1989

THE CHURCHES OF CHINA, Taking Root Downward, Bearing Fruit Upward. 1986, 1987, 1990 (Translated into German, 1987)

BAPTISTS AROUND THE WORLD, Albert W. Warden, Editor
(section on China). 1995

CHRISTIANITY IN TODAY'S CHINA:
The story of the churches of China continues:
Taking root downward, bearing fruit upward.

For information E-mail: The Tao Foundation, <bet@laotao.org>
See the Internet web sites: <www.laotao.org/tao> &
                                    <www.laotao.org/mission>

CONTENTS

FOREWORD
by David M. Paton,
China missionary and author of
Christian Missions and the Judgment of God

I am grateful to be allowed the privilege of contributing a short foreword to Britt Towery's book on the churches of today's China.

There is an increasing number of books on the Church in China today. Some are scholarly or written by skilled and reliable journalist or people knowledgeable about the Church in the People's Republic. But the majority of these books are not of good quality, and some it would be hard to call honest. The Evangelical churches of the North Atlantic find it difficult to believe that the Church in China is alive and vigorous.

Britt Towery is a leading figure in the Southern Baptist Convention Foreign Mission Board. The book is an informal account by an American mission official from Texas of how China and the Chinese Church strike him today.

Unlike many Evangelicals, he seems not unduly worried by Communism, nor does he need to bolster his distaste for it by vastly exaggerating the size of the "underground" churches. There are a lot of conversations with Chinese that Britt Towery has met in China, and there is also information about all the theological seminaries, the structures of the churches, and so on. Informal as it is, it still has down to earth things like bibliography, chronology, religious documents and imagination.

"Taking root downward, bearing fruit upward" is a very good description of the last forty years. I hope that it will be read widely.

David M. Paton,
Gloucester, England
1989

INTRODUCTION
to a continuing story:
The miracle and challenge of God's churches in China

Behold, these shall come from far; and low, these from the north and from the west; and these from the land of Sinim. Sing, O heavens; and be joyful, O earth; And break forth into singing, O mountains; for the Lord hath comforted his people, And will have mercy upon his afflicted.

---Isaiah 49:12-13

The last quarter of the 20th century has been one of the brightest and most exciting periods for Christianity in China. Yet it is almost an unknown story. There is more mis-information and dis-information on the churches and the believers than actual on the scene reports.

This book is written from the inside. From China with the thoughts, dreams and spirit of the pastors and laity that have taken on the challenge of making Christianity in China "Chinese."

The challenge of making Christianity in China meet the needs of the people and nation. They are meeting that challenge by word and deed that China needs Christianity. Not the western variety and theology but a pattern and spirit that is born from the very soil and hope of the people themselves.

Biblical scholars have disagreed through the centuries over the location of the land of Sinim mentioned in the above biblical reference by the Old Testament prophet Isaiah. But most seemed to be of the opinion that ancient Sinim mentioned here in the Hebrew Bible is actually much of what we today call China.

None disagree though that the rest of the passage applies to today's China. There has been a great out pouring of God's grace on the people of that vast land. Bibles are being published;

new churches are being built or old ones re-opened, home worship centers expanding; seminaries developed in major population areas; and more and more simple freedoms to live and breath and worship as never before in half a century.

Earlier editions of this work under the title "The Churches of China" (1986, 1987, 1990) have long been out of print and out of date.

This book was begun with the hope it would help Western peoples, readers of English, to enter into the China churches joys and victories. There has been so much disinformation and half-truths about Christians in China that such a book like this was necessary.

There have been persecutions of religious bodies in China. But they are isolated incidents and not government policy. They are not a part of the Communist Party's plot to destroy Christianity or religion in general. Christians, while numbering over 20 million (no one really knows how many are in China), they are still a minority that does not apparently worry the Party leaders.

The West's understanding of China is very limited. Few give it much thought or care. It is so far away, and that language is impossible! It is an old civilization, over 5,000 years of recorded history. In many ways it is so far behind much of the modern world.

Things are changing fast. Over 40,000 Chinese from the China mainland are studying in American universities and schools at any given time. They are learning about us, the good and bad. We in America need to catch up and learn more about the Chinese and China.

The book is divided into two parts. (The bamboo art work for Part One, Part Two and the cover were done by my wife, Jody. She is one of the finest non-Chinese to paint Chinese scenes. And a Texas girl, she has no equal when it comes to preparing Chinese food!)

Part One is eleven chapters that sketch church history in China and how the churches of the 1990s came to be what they are today; where they came from -- and possibly where they are going.

Part Two lists by province selected churches that the visitor may visit, learn about and intercede in prayer for them. There are also interesting pieces on each province that helps to introduce the area to those who have never been there or read much about the geography of China. This second part of the book evolved from a prayer list. On one of my first visits to the offices of the Three-Self Patriotic Movement Committee in Shanghai, I asked if I might have a list of Shanghai area churches and their addresses. When I told Pastor Shen Cheng'en my reasons, he prepared a list for me. Pastor Shen is the editor of the monthly church magazine *Tian Feng* (Heavenly Breezes).

Above all, I want to deepen the reader's interest and knowledge of China as it exists today. I want more Christians to be praying for the peoples of China.

When China Christians are asked how the outsiders might help them, they have always replied, "Pray for us." Nothing will be more valuable to the Kingdom of God in China than this.

Though the biblical phrase used as the sub-title of this book is referring to the remnant of the house of Judah I believe it can also be said of the remnant of the whole house of God in China during this century. For the churches are really *taking* root downward into the soil, soul and society and they are continuing to *bear* fruit upward to the glory of God.

This book is a popular account of what I have seen and experienced. It is not an exhaustive or comprehensive story of Christiananity in China. No one book could hold all the varied experiences of the many people of China and their individual and group encounters with Christ. This account does not pretend to even cover the Protestants and barely touches the work of the Catholics. Nor is there a great deal about the tremendous response to Christ among the many minorities of China. I have not included the footnotes that were in earlier editions, but I have expanded the reading list to include many views of China Christianity, religion and history the reader might want to pursue.

My primary purpose is to introduce the reader to a portion of the trail the Christians have walked in recent years. I hope it will increase the army of "pray-ers" for the peoples of China.

Britt Towery
Waco, Texas USA

January 12, 2000

Part One

CHAPTER ONE

Seeking Forgiveness and Reconciliation

"Be kind to one another, tender-hearted, forgiving each other, just as God in Christ has forgiven you."
--Ephesians 4:32

The Christian churches of the China mainland began the year 2000 with seventeen seminaries and numerous Bible colleges and short-term lay Bible schools. The training of a new generation of church workers has grown slowly but surely since the end of the infamous "Cultural Revolution" that began in 1966 and took ten years to wind down. It will be many generations before the emotional and spiritual scars of those years are somewhat forgotten.

In 1979 when Christians began seeking to re-open their churches there was a concerted effort to train preachers. There had been no formal training for church workers since the late 1950s. Now the leadership that remained was old. Men who never thought they might preach again were called back to help open the churches and begin some kind of training for the young who felt the call of God to minister.

The story of the China seminaries comes later. This story reveals the hearts of a former Red Guard and a seminary professor. Two people from two different worlds and experiences brought together in the tragedy that was the "Cultural Revolution." The following story took place just after the Jinling (another name for the city of Nanjing) Theological Seminary began classes again. It is a true story related to me by my Hong Kong and China colleague in the 1980s, Charles Wilson.

The entrance to the Jinling Theological Seminary in Nanjing is on the small Da Jian Yin Lane near the heart of the old city. Soon after the school had reopened in the spring of 1981, a

3

young man in his late twenties or early thirties walked down that small lane to the gate of the seminary. His eyes showed fear, yet there was a resolution to finish what he had begun.

He expected to be stopped by the gateman. Any stranger is stopped when entering unannounced at any gate in China.

"Please," he said to the gateman, "I must see someone here."

The old gateman had seen many a student come and go through these gates. In recent years, tourists -- especially those with Christian insights and connections -- came this way to see China's only national Protestant seminary. This distraught stranger did not look much different from the hundreds of young people in Nanjing: white shirt and blue cotton pants, well-worn sandals -- pretty much the wardrobe of most Chinese young people for more than a generation. He wore no socks, which would put him in the best circles among some fashion-conscious Westerners.

The gateman, knowing this young man was not a tourist or a student, turned to a little boy inside the gate house and sent him through the hedges to the administration building straight ahead. The visitor, still waiting at the gate, began to show signs of nervous anxiety, even of indecision -- yet he felt he could not relax until he had said his piece to someone inside.

The sun was bright, even though it was now late afternoon. Nanjing already was beginning to experience an early summer. This former Treaty Port city, along with Chongqing and Wuhan, is known as one of the three furnaces of China. Nanjing means "the southern capital," and for several of China's dynasties it served as the nation's capital. The first Ming emperors are buried here, as is the founder of the Republic of China, Dr. Sun Yat Sen (Sun Zhongshan).

From the front steps of the main building the little boy caught the gatekeeper's eye. Beside the boy was a man in his late sixties. In that instant, the white-shirted and blue-trousered visitor walked hurriedly toward the building. It was evident the young man had been there before -- but not under these circumstances. He looked neither to the left nor to the right but directly ahead at the elderly man on the steps. As he got to the building he stopped, and his eyes and head went down. He

4

stared at his dirty sandals. His hands were unable to find anything to do. He blurted out his name, begging the pardon for such an intrusion, and asked to speak to someone in authority.

The elderly professor came down the steps and asked the young visitor to come inside out of the sun.

"But," the young man said to the teacher, "can you forgive me?"

"What, my son, is it you want forgiven?"

Then in a dialogue too sacred to repeat word for word, the young man sank down on the steps and began to explain why he had come and why he sought their forgiveness. It had been at least fifteen years since he had been on those steps, on this campus. As he sat there now, with his head in his hands, his confession revealed the torment of his soul. He looked up and said: "I helped burn your books, your library..." He wanted to say more but could not.

As the young man tried to talk, the professor helped him up and took him inside to a parlor usually used to entertain visitors of another sort. Before the stranger would sit down, he asked again, "Can I be forgiven for such a crime?" The professor let him pour out his heart about those days so long ago and yet still so close -- a time when China's youth were taken down a dead-end street that almost led to destruction of an entire generation and nearly took the country down the drain with them.

Of all the horrors Westerners and the Japanese had heaped upon China for the last two centuries, none was as traumatic or far-reaching as the lawless years of the "Cultural Revolution" and what the Chinese did to themselves.

This young man was like so many whose hearts condemned them for the errors and excesses of Mao Zedong's mania to remain in power under any circumstances. The Great Proletarian Cultural Revolution, as it was officially called, burst forth in May, 1966, and was directed primarily against those in the Communist Party, Mao said, who had begun taking the capitalist road. The youth of the country were used by Jiang Qing, Mao Zedong's fourth and last wife, to fulfill her desires to become the Empress of all China. Bourgeois educated people were suspect. Anyone with foreign connections was in trouble. Cultural institutions -- including Christian churches and religious structures -- were found guilty overnight of being harmful to China's future. Lawlessness became the law of the land. In sheer terror it reached far deeper than had any wars, purges or traumas of the 19th and 20th centuries.

The Gang of Four, as they came to be known (Jiang Qing, Zhang Chunqiao, Yao Wenyuan, and Wang Hongwen), used Mao's overestimation of the danger of revisionism by calling for the eradication of the "Four Olds," namely old ideas, old culture, old customs, and old habits. Although the worst period was 1966-69, the misery was to extend to a full ten years -- and even longer in the memory. Not until the death of Mao and the arrest of the Gang of Four did sanity and common sense begin to show signs of a return in the land of China.

The professor sat quietly as the young man sought peace of mind and soul in the re-telling of the events of the night when he and other young Chinese had burned the seminary library, book by book.

It was not a pleasant memory for the aging professor. He well remembered the day the Red Guards came on campus. They were going to set up their headquarters in the seminary buildings. The school was one of the best built, best maintained structures in the whole city. Long before it was the site of China's first college for women. The seminary and grounds were coveted by two Red Guard units -- both attempting to rid Nanjing of the "Four Olds."

At first the Red Guard leader gave them 48 hours to save as many books as they could. This concession was given only when it was urged upon the intruders that many of the books were good for China and could not be replaced. As several teachers worked well into the night seeking to find and preserve the most valuable books, the Red Guards came with new instructions. As the saying goes, they liked to cut off a dog's tail by inches.

Looking around the stacks of books and seeing the flurry of activity to save some, the Red Guards said, "We do not have 48 hours to wait. Get what you want of these books in 24 hours!"

As the deadline approached, about 5,000 volumes were shuttled off to storage places. Then, countless books that can never be replaced were thrown from the windows by the Red Guards and dumped into a pile for burning. It had been hard for anyone there to forget the devilish glee those young people had that night as they put the torch to the books piled high in front of the administration building.

It was a time when all of China was caught up in the frenzy of uncontrolled youth -- youth goaded by those in power, youth who were encouraged and assured that what they were doing would bring forth a better, purer China.

"We were wrong, we were led astray," the young man said, as he looked up to find the professor offering him a cup of tea.

"Yes," said the professor as he sat opposite the young man. "Those were days when wrong became right, and right became wrong. Nothing made sense. No one knew what was going on."

Then the professor shifted his feet and got to the heart of the matter: "As to your question--yes, you are forgiven. All of us are sinners. We are forgiven sinners. God's grace in Christ Jesus has taken away our sin and guilt. Our Bible says he has taken our sins as far as the east is from the west, ... so has God separated our sins from us. It is not something we deserve. It is God's grace to all mankind."

How much, professor Chen Zemin thought, as he looked at the boy, does this young man understand of what I am saying? Regardless, he knew he must help him with the whole truth, so he added: "With such a forgiving God, it is not for us to withhold that same forgiving grace from you."

Whether the young man fully understood or became a Christian believer after that visit or began to worship in one of Nanjing's three churches or one of the many home assembly gathering points (often called 'house churches' in the West), no one knows. But he did get the main lesson of the Christian faith. He learned that God was in Christ reconciling the world unto himself. The heart of reconciliation is forgiveness. Many in China, as in the world, continue to grapple with this reality, for it has not been easy -- following the turmoil of the "Cultural Revolution" -- for families to be reconciled, nor easy for Christians to forgive Christians. Those were days of testing and

7

trial that few people of any faith have ever been called upon to endure.

The ill feeling and resentment, even the great sense of emptiness and helplessness, are evident even today in many homes and villages, and among the Christian people, as well. Many lives, many hopes and dreams, shattered. Many families and communities are still in pieces twenty-five years later. For there can be no peace of mind and heart without reconciliation.

That is why the primary message of the churches of China the last two decades has been on building mutual respect among believers and non-believers, letting their Chinese neighbors and government know that Christians are good for the country. That Christians and non-Christians have suffered together and now must learn to live together, "forgetting what is behind, pressing on to what is before." That was what professor Chen Zemin was sharing with the repentant, former Red Guard.

More on the Red Guards and the years of the "Cultural Revolution" in Chapter Four. The next chapter is a brief survey of the Protestant venture into China beginning in the seventh century and a brief look at the problems and joys Protestants encounter 1807 to 1950.

CHAPTER TWO

Western Beginnings, 1807-1954
A Summary of Missionary History in China

Jesus once said to his disciples
"As the Father has sent me, I also send you."
--- John 20:21

God's people have always been stronger after times of stress, and the Christians of China have emerged from the "Cultural Revolution" with a deep personal experience of the presence, power and grace of the Lord Jesus Christ in a way that few believers in history ever encounter. One passage of scripture that was constantly exchanged among Christians during those days was Psalm 23:4, "Yea, though I walk through the valley of the shadow of death, I will fear no evil; for Thou art with me; Thy rod and Thy staff they comfort me."

Soon after the closing days of the Cultural Revolution, some of the Christian leaders met and sent a letter with this verse of comfort to all the Christians of China. To this day when you meet Christians they refer to those dark days in the context of this verse from the Psalms. Their God had walked with them through a terror that blew the minds and hearts of even the mighty and strong. It was not like anything the Christians -- and all Chinese -- had ever experienced before.

Historically, Protestant churches seldom found it an easy task to be the witness the masses of China demanded. The Christian message has been used and abused by Chinese and foreigners alike over the past two centuries. The difference in the China experience is at the point of the missionary's entry and association with evils that have nothing to do with the message of the man of Galilee. These unnecessary weights continue to burden the pure and simple message of Christ and cause it to be distorted by many who know nothing of its true spirit and power.

Records left by the *Jingjiao*, a Syrian sect, that Western historians have called Nestorians, reveal accounts of Christianity in China in the seventh century A.D.

In the year 1625 a ten foot tall stone monument of these Syrians was uncovered near Chang'an, the present city of Xi'an. This stone monument called the Nestorian Tablet records the history, theology and names of the early Syrian believers who settled in Tang dynasty China. It is on permanent exhibition in the Shaanxi Museum in Xi'an.

These Tang dynasty Syrian believers called themselves *Jingjiao* which means "Religion of Light." This is a much better Chinese name for the Christian faith than either of the present terms used by the Catholics or the Protestants. Dr. Peter C. H. Chiu, former church history professor at the Hong Kong Baptist Theological Seminary, in his writings explains how the name Jingjiao fits Christianity so beautifully -- for did not Jesus say he was the "Light of the world." (C.H. Chiu. *An Historical Study of Nestorian Christianity in the Tang Dynasty Between A.D, 635-845,* Ph.D. dissertation, Southwestern Baptist Theological Seminary, Fort Worth, Texas, USA, 1987).

In spite of the Jingjiao follower's efforts, Christianity remained foreign by Chinese standards -- while, at the same time, Buddhism from India and Islam from Arab countries were fast becoming known as Chinese religions. Islam gained such a stronghold that today the followers of Mohammed are one of the strongest of China's ethnic minorities, called the Hui Nationality.

After the *Jingjiao* suffered setbacks through persecution they scattered across China, most going to Mongolia where they were well received. Many of the descendents of these Jingjiao believers returned to China when Genghis Khan's (1162?-1227) descendents set up the Yuan dynasty (1271-1368).

The Jingjiao or desecendents of the Nestorians spread the Christian faith among the Keraits (sometimes spelled Kereyid) to such an extend that by the early eleventh century they were known as a Christian tribe. In the thirteenth century the chief of the Keraits had become the primary leader of the Mongols. He was Yesugei, father of Genghis Khan.

10

A daughter-in-law of Genghis Khan, Sorkaktani (Sorkaktani-beki), was a Nestorian Christian, and mother of three sons who became emperors. The most noteworthy for our study was her son, Kublai Khan, the first emperor of the Yuan dynasty in China from 1260 to 1294. (For more on Christians in ancient Mongolia see *The Successors of Genghis Khan*, translated by J. A. Boyle, 1970, Columbia University Press, pages 168-170 and *The History of the Mongol Conquests* by J. J. Saunders.)

By the end of the sixteenth century Jesuit missionaries followed the Portuguese explorers in another introduction of Christianity to China. Most notable of these was Matteo Ricci (1552-1610) who tried to mold Catholicism into Chinese thought. But by 1776 the Jesuits were limited to little if any religious activity. The Western religious philosophies did not take root all over China. In some areas there were lasting impressions and results that can be seen today. In Sichuan province toward the end of the eighteenth century there were from two to three hundred thousand Catholics that came from the Jesuits missionary work. Many and varied are the Christian-related books now published in Sichuan.

Christianity was introduced again to China at the beginning of the nineteenth century -- this time from the south rather than across the deserts of the north and northwest. For some 40 years (1800-1840), men and women from Western nations made slight incursions in and around the south China port of Guangzhou and the Portuguese enclave of Macau. Most notable were men like Robert Morrison (born January 5, 1782, died August 1, 1834) and Karl Friedrich August (Charles) Gutzlaff (born July 8, 1803, died August 9, 1851). Both were able men who unfortunately had little knowledge of China or the Chinese people. They were walking trails few foreigners had ever walked before. They had to write their own language text books and make their own strategy. Both these men worked for companies that forced opium on the Chinese nation. Both men were involved with and employed by countries that contrived the unequal treaties imposed upon the dragon throne. This made it difficult for succeeding generations of Chinese to separate the foreigners

11

who traded in opium from the foreigners with the Christian gospel story.

Foreign powers began their move into China in the early nineteenth century, just as they had in Africa, India and other parts of Asia. From the 1840s onward the colonization of the Chinese ports became even easier by the gradual demise of the Qing Dynasty. The Manchus never equaled the earlier Tang, Song or Ming dynasties. The last sixty years for the Qing (Manchu) dynasty saw little effort at reform and growing hatred for the more powerful Western nations. The decline had set in and would cease only in 1911 with the formation of Sun Yat-sen's republican form of government.

The missionary work and foreign imperialism expanded with little regard to Chinese law or custom. Both the opium traffic and the missionary work were under the protection of the foreign governments and above Chinese law. This fact of history has not been lost on the present government of China. Every time Christians from Hong Kong or the West smuggle Bibles or Christian literature into China, they are telling the Chinese government and Communist Party officials in Beijing that Christianity is still a foreign religion and is still above the Chinese law. Such actions make the Chinese Christians suspect in the eyes of the unbelieving and unknowing officials.

The Treaty of Nanjing in 1842 was the first of the unequal treaties that Britain forced on the Manchus. Hong Kong island was ceded to the British. This did not go unnoticed by the rest of the European community. The Treaties of Tianjin (1858) and later Beijing (1860) made possible the opening of ten additional Chinese ports to foreign residents. Until this time foreigners could not legally travel to the interior. Now they could travel anywhere in China as they so desired. This "toleration clause," as it came to be known, made the spread of the faith legal; but it was "at the point of a bayonet." (Stephen Neill. *Colonialism and Christian Mission*, New York: McGraw-Hill, 1966, p. 139)

K. S. Latourette wrote in the 1920s: "This provision [Tianjin and Beijing treaties] in part removed Chinese Christians from the jurisdiction of Chinese officials, for any alleged persecution could be referred by the missionaries to a consul or minister for presentation to the imperial authorities. It led to abuses, because not infrequently Chinese professed conversion to obtain the assistance of the missionary and the consul in lawsuits." (Kenneth Scott Latourette, *The Chinese, Their History and Culture*. New York: Macmillian, 1961, p. 283)

Very little protest is found in the writings of the missionaries of those days. There was protest to be sure. The few protests that were made of these injustices could not be heard above the clamor of the foreigner's greed for power and control over the sleeping dragon.

True Christianity survived in China because God had a higher purpose than any man could imagine. The church had to be Chinese to gain the respect of the nation. The Chinese church had to become Chinese from the inside out. When I went to see the movie "Gandhi" in Hong Kong, the one part of the film that brought loud applause was when the Mahatma told the British that, after Indians take over India, "We will make mistakes, but they will be Indian mistakes." The Chinese would rather make the mistakes in China today than to continue having the foreigners making them. This is one of the painful truths of growing into self-respecting nationhood.

One spring day in 1847, a son of the southern province of Guangdong made his way down to the capital city of Guangzhou (Canton) to learn more of the Christian faith. Hong Xiuquan (Hung Hsiu-ch'uan, 1814-1864) was his name and he had been twice before as a candidate for an advanced degree in the government civil service examinations. Twice he had failed and remained a village school teacher. After his last failure he came into contact with Christianity.

Hong said he heard a foreign missionary with a long white beard and a Chinese interpreter preaching on the street. He paused but only for a moment. He accepted some pamphlets which were written by Liang Fa and returned to his village north of Guangzhou. Liang Fa (1789-1855) was the first Chinese Christian minister of the modern era and assistant to Robert Morrison.

Hong put these pamphlets aside when he returned to his village. Some time later his interest in them was rekindled after he experienced weird dreams and visions that gave him problems.

On a March day in 1847, along with his cousin Hong Rengan, he returned to Guangzhou and sought out the American Southern Baptist missionary, I. J. Roberts (born February 17, 1802, died January 4, 1871). Roberts, along with fellow Baptist Jehu Lewis Shuck (1812-1863), had earlier been the first missionaries to begin a church in the new British Colony of Hong Kong. One of the two churches these men began in Hong Kong was located in the heart of the island's present financial district on the corner of Ice House Street and Queen's Road Central. After Shuck's wife, Henrietta Hall, died (she was the first foreign woman buried in the new British colony of Hong Kong at Happy Valley) and Roberts moved to Canton, the Baptists lost what today is some of the world's most valuable property -- "smack dab" in the heart of downtown Victoria on Hong Kong Island.

Hong Xiuquan received some Christian principles, more biblical scriptures and a few spiritual truths from his brief stay with Roberts. What he learned seemed to confirm his strange dreams. He felt assured he could make a difference in his world. Roberts, not alert to the possibilities of Hong, decided against baptizing him or training him further.

Feng Yunshan had organized what he called the Society of God-Worshippers and Idol Smashers. Hong Xiuquan took over the movement and developed it into the *Taiping Tianguo,* the Kingdom of Heavenly Peace (1851-1864). Foreign businessmen and missionaries liked what they heard of the Taiping Revolution as it made its way through South China to Nanjing (killing millions and recruiting others along the way). There in the ancient capital of China, Hong set up his semi-Christian kingdom and throne. When it became evident the Taipings might rule China and deprive the West of their treaty ports and special privileges, the foreigners no longer cared for Hong and sent in their armies to help the Manchus finally crush the movement.

The red-turbaned, long-haired Taipings were the hope of many Chinese for more than 15 years. They had never liked the foreign Manchu rule and this was the largest of many revolts on the Qing dynasty of the hated Manchus. Had the inner decay and outer pressure been less, the outcome would have been different. Taiping laws were far ahead of the laws of that day in China. The end came as Nanjing began to crumble. On June 1, 1864, Hong Xiuquan died at the age of 51 after a lingering illness. The best study of the movement is Jen Yu-wen's *The Taiping Revolution*, Yale University Press, 1973. The best study of Hong is Jonathan Spence's *God's Chinese Son*, Norton, 1996.

Nearly a generation later, as the twentieth century began to dawn, another people's movement emerged. The Boxers or *Yihetuan* (righteous fists) were unlike the Taipings. They wanted to rid China of the foreigners. Since most foreigners were Christian missionaries they suffered the most. They believed in weird magic and proclaim foreign bullets could not hurt them.

Thousands of Chinese Christians and 230 foreign missionaries and their children were killed. The British Missionary Society lost the most personnel. In Taiyuan, Shanxi province, the governor called the foreigners from the countryside to the court and cut off their heads one at a time.

Once again foreign troops pushed into China to put down this fanatical uprising. The Christian missionary movement suffered most as it became evident that the churches of China, after one hundred years of work, were still viewed as foreign and anything but Chinese in origin or custom. (For more on those years see: *A Thousand miles of miracle in China* by A. E. Glover, CIM Press, 1857, and *Dragon Lady* by Sterling Seagrave, Vintage Press, 1992.)

A Chinese Christian friend in China, whose mother was a small girl during the time of the Boxer Rebellion, gave me new insight into those days of chaos and insight from the Chinese point of view. His mother being from a Christian family, was sent to Beijing to attend a mission school. The Boxers were in control of Beijing. The leaders of the mission school brought the children together to pray for deliverance. They prayed for the foreign troops who were headed for Beijing. They prayed that the foreign soldiers would defeat her own people! Unwittingly the missionaries were setting the Chinese against themselves, and the Christian message of reconciliation and love had taken a

15

back seat again. Even though this was not the intent of the missionaries, it was the historical result.

The missionary movement in the first half of the twentieth century in China survived the 1911 revolution which followed the Boxer uprising and brought down the Qing Dynasty. Missionaries witnessed the founding of the Republic of China -- only to be caught up in local warlord banditry and the growing division between the Nationalist Party and the Communist Party. In the 1920s more schools and hospitals were begun and more missionaries came from around the world to minister to a nation with more problems than solutions. Much of the time from 1927 to 1949 China was in the throes of an undeclared civil war.

During those years many of the missionaries did not take sides. Many did. The majority of the Protestant missionaries were anti-Communist. Few foreign missionaries had any first-hand knowledge of the national issues China was facing. A number of them served as interpreters for the Nationalist forces during World War II and were honored by the Nationalist government. Few Southern Baptist missionaries, to my knowledge, made efforts to know or understand the Communist leaders and what was behind their whole scheme. When something is dismissed out of hand, it is not learned. Most Western missionaries had witnessed enough to assure them that the Communist Party was from the devil himself. *Time Magazine* and former missionaries like Walter Judd spread the word about the evils of the Party. *Time Magazine* was founded by the son of Presbytern missionaries to China.

With the end of the Chinese Civil War in 1949, a new day dawned over China. Many thought it was for the best. The Nationalists government had been so corrupt the people would have chosen anything to avoid more of Chiang Kai-shek's rule. It is best expressed by the statement Mao Zedong made on October 1st that year at the founding of the People's Republic of China (PRC) in Beijing: "The Chinese people have stood up!"

The ability to stand when one has been held down so long is not easy and takes time. Now, 50 years later, through struggle and chaos, off and on progress, a New China continues to try and rise from the ashes. The emerging church of China must be viewed through these years of turmoil. To miss these changes and what brought them about is to miss the deeper meaning of all that is taking place in the Christian community in China today. Just as China attempts to modernize and catch up with the 20th century before it ends, so the church seeks to be a Chinese church in form and spirit.

With the founding of the PRC, many missionaries who were openly favorable to the Nationalists' cause, left China. Others stayed on to do what they could under the new government. Southern Baptist missionaries Polly and Glenn Morris stayed on in Shanghai after the liberation but soon found they could do less and less normal missionary work. Another Southern Baptist, Pearl Johnson of South Carolina, was told in Qingdao that her presence was becoming more of a hindrance than a help to the Baptist believers there. Pearl was the last Southern Baptist missionary to leave China after the liberation.

Those were difficult days for everyone. Most Communists viewed the churches and Christianity as foreign-dominated. Not knowing any missionaries personally, it is understandable that some Communist intentionally or unintentionally viewed the missionaries as working in China for their own government or own interests rather than for religious reasons. Once again the far-right-leaning Harry Luce and his *Time Magazine* propaganda had called the Communist devils many times. And Luce's praise of the Nationalist's Chiang Kai-shek went too far. (See *In Search of History* by Theodore H. White, Harper and Row, 1978.)

With the outbreak of the Korean War in June, 1950, relations with foreigners were strained even further in China. Missionaries and Chinese Christians were generally accused of being spies and traitors.

Feng Jiasheng (known as Charlie Feng to missionary friends) was the son of the first Baptist pastor in the city of Suzhou. He was a teacher in Hujiang University (known as Shanghai University to the missionary community) an American-Southern Baptist sponsored college -- a school the Communists felt was not as helpful as it should have been in the revolution. Feng spent seven years at hard labor in the distant

17

province of Anhui, followed by 13 years of house arrest. Such injustices are slowly being redressed. Feng Jiasheng was absolved, finally, of all his "crimes" and declared innocent by the courts in 1985 (See Feng and his family in portion of the ABC-Radio-TV Commission Emmy-award-winning documentary "China: Walls and Bridges").

Another Chinese friend I met in 1984, Pastor Han Chongyi, of Kaifeng, had to take charge of the foreign mission work when the Southern Baptist missionaries left his area in 1949. In the 1950s he was even turned in and falsely accused by one of his own Baptist co-workers and spent ten years in prison.

In this period of confusion, China, trying to set up a workable government and fight America in Korea at the same time, a new church began to emerge in China. It was felt by most Christian leaders of the 1950s that they must separate themselves from the age-old foreign label. It appeared to these Chinese Christians that they would have better opportunities among their own people if they made a definite break from missionary dependence to independence.

After the Christian Manifesto of September 23, 1950, was signed and circulated, the Three-Self Patriotic Movement was instituted at the First National Christian Conference of China in 1954. This was not an original idea peculiar to China Christians. In various countries of the world the desire for self-governing, self-supporting and self-propagating churches had been heard.

Many China missionaries made efforts in this direction. Numerous independent churches developed in China without any ties to foreign mission groups or missionaries. The Three-Self principle is one of Baptists' most cherished ideals: the autonomy of the local church -- the right of believers to worship through their own experience in their own culture and custom.

The Three-Self Movement is seen by many as the Chinese Christians' effort to live down the bad side of missionary endeavor -- so that they may open up the lines of communication with the Chinese people in a new and fresh way. This to some appears to be nationalistic and anti-foreign. K. H. Ting replies: "The Three-Self Movement's aim is limited to achieving a Chinese identity for the churches in China. That is, they are to be just as Chinese as churches in England are English and those in the U.S.A. are American. Churches with a Chinese identity are still a part -- indeed a better part -- of the Universal Church. We only wish to stop being merely a dot on the missionary map of Western churches. Only then can we begin to bring enrichment in the Universal Church."

The image of the Three-Self Movement in the 1980s was hampered and haunted by its image made in the 1950s. In trying to unify the churches of China in the 1950s and in trying to get away from the foreign label, many grassroots Christians did not understand nor see the bigger picture. The changes often came too fast and with mixed motives.

Three-Self leadership saw the advantages of such unity long before it was understood by most believers. Many even today have no intention of forgetting their denominational heritage. Compounding the problem in some counties and provinces were Three-Self personnel who undertook their tasks more like feudal overseers than as understanding Christian shepherds.

As Mao's Great Leap Forward got underway in 1958 the churches began to feel the Communist Party's wrath. Many churches in large cities were merged. Attendance was down in all churches. People were busy with their backyard iron furnaces trying to enhance the production of everything. The government began to use church property for warehouses, factories, schools. Hence a city that had 30 or 40 churches was cut to having four or five. Many villages were left without any place of worship. A history of those hectic days has yet to be written. It is my opinion that only a Chinese who lived through it can write it. There are no simple explanations to the decades of the fifties and sixties in China. Everyone was walking a new road.

The Cultural Revolution (1966-76) resulted in the first real unity among Christians. It was a unity that no man-made decree could forge. Denominations were of little importance for the Christians and all the peoples of China had suffered together during those traumatic years. As one survivor of the Cultural Revolution said of his pastor, "We worked and ate together, we wept and laughed together. We grew together, and pastors today in China are not like they were before. The good ones are better and the best ones even greater." Then he said what many have told me: "Nothing good came from those lost years, except they brought us closer to God and the realities of life."

This brief overview of Christian missions in China, primarily the modern era of 1807 to 1954, from the arrival of the first foreign missionary to the first National Christian Conference, does not do justice to the heroic witness of foreigners and Chinese Christians alike during those years. Many stories have been remembered and written but they only scratch the surface of the planting and re-planting of Christianity in Chinese soil.

Finally in the 1980s, after nearly 200 years of Christian activity, China's Christian believers did what many had wanted to do for a long time but warlords, famines and revolution had kept them from accomplishing it. They saw the need to rid their churches of the label that kept many Chinese from church, "the foreign religion" label.

Given time to grow the Christian experience in China can become the salt and light many of the older churches and denominations of the world need. Any study of history that does not result in a new vision for the future, attainable or not, is wasted effort.

What has become known as the Postdenominational era in China Christianity merely means that the Christians of China see the importance of being one not only in spirit but in reality. Hence they do not have Western denominational names over their churches. They are thankful for their Baptist or Methodist or Presbyterian heritage but that is all it is to them now. They are simply "Christian Churches." Not an easy road to walk but vital if the churches are to continue to grow.

This means the Western Christian must seek to find an honest and open way to work with their Chinese brethren. It is not a time to be in competition with the China Christian Council or local Chinese churches. Some American mission boards continue to carry on covert operations in China. This is unfortunate. For it misleads the Chinese Communist Party and government to thinking that Christians are still the enemy and do not have to obey the laws of the land. It is a moral law: work with the local Christians to enhance the faith and grow Chinese (not Baptist or foreign) churches.

As the year 2007 approaches and Western and China Protestants celebrate 200 years of the modern missionary movement in their land may it be a time of rejoicing -- rejoicing that the foreign missionary brought them the gospel in the first place; but more rejoicing for the new ways God has allowed them to grow; and rejoicing that Christians in China are finally viewed as good citizens and important to the nation; rejoicing that in the new century their western brothers and sisters will work with them as equals and friends, rather than as mission board directors.

For those mission societies and missionaries that would turn the clock back, to what some call, the "good old days," let it go back farther than the days of Morrison and Gutzlaff, let the 21st century missionaries turn the clock back all the way to the first century and let the Lord Jesus himself be the model. He said it best himself: "Whoever wishes to be first among you shall be your slave; just as the Son of Man did not come to be served, but to serve..."(Matthew 20:27, 28).

But before that can be there must be a better understanding of the years that followed the foreign missionary's leaving China in 1950. And the next chapter seeks to look at those years of a new beginning, 1949-1960.

CHAPTER THREE

The Years of New Beginnings, 1949-1960

I will put a new spirit within you..."
--- Ezekiel 11:19

The year 1949 was not only near the end of the first half of the 20th century but near the end of a long and bitter struggle for the control of a quarter of the world's population.

In 1911 the Republic of China was formed out of the ruins of the aging and powerless Manchu-led Qing dynasty. Sun Yat-sen (1866-1925) the Father of the Republic, built on the work of reformers like Kang Youwei (1859-1927), led the way in founding the new republic.

Sun had no power base in the north so he moved the nation's capital from Peking (Beijing) to Nanking (Nanjing). Sun resigned as president and his Nationalist Party (KMT or Kuomintang) floundered even more. It was a case of too many chiefs and not enough Indians. Some wanted to bring back the dynasty. Yuan Shikai (1859-1916), one-time general for the Empress Dowager and would-be emperor, saw to his own needs rather than those of the new nation. Very few people even knew what the word democracy meant, fewer still saw any need for it.

Long before he became the world famous reformer Dr. Sun lived in Macau, the Portuguese possession west of Hong Kong. It is not commonly known but his wife during those more peaceful days was an active member of the Baptist Church on White Horse Road. Later he was to marry Charlie Soong's daughter Soong Ching Ling (Song Qingling).

As World War I was winding down in Europe Japan extended her domain in China by taking possession of the German-leased Shandong coastline. After the great war China was unable to regain this territory Japan had taken illegally. The Shandong coastline should have been returned to China after Germany's defeat. Western powers at Versailles allowed Japan to keep it. When Japan made more demands of China Beijing University students, rightly feeling they could no longer trust the western powers, protested to their Nationalist government for being so weak. The protest began on May 4, 1919. The May Fourth Movement, as it came to be called, began the end of China's domination by western powers. It ushered in a new era in Chinese history.

A direct result of the May Fourth Movement was the birth of the Chinese Communist Party on July 1, 1921.

The Christian community in China in the 1920s had reached its zenith as far as numbers of believers and foreign missionaries. The majority of the missionaries were teachers in the growing number of Christian colleges and middle schools. Intellectuals in China saw the desperate need for education but were leery of the foreign element so pronounced in the mission schools.

Southern Baptist missionary activity was primarily in the provinces of Shandong, Henan, Jiangsu, Guangdong and the city of Shanghai during these years. Schools were usually named after a former missionary, marking Christianity even more as a foreign religion. English was a major part of the curriculum, often to the exclusion of Chinese culture and custom. A great deal of good was accomplished through the Western-oriented education. Many Chinese were challenged in mind, but few in heart. Though many missionaries hoped Christianity would take root in China through schools and medical institutions it just did not happen.

There were many missionaries and Chinese leaders longing for the day that Christianity would take root in the hearts of the people and nation. As mission schools had to give more and more attention to academics and less time to evangelism the schools grew away from the churches just as they did in America's original thirteen colonies.

Most of the Christian believers in the churches were not well educated. Many were hard working honest peasants but were not the leaders in their villages or areas. Thus the missionaries themselves led the churches too long. They were slow to give the care of the churches to the Chinese.

There were so many demands, all urgent, upon the understaffed mission stations. The one thing many wanted, growing an effective Chinese church in Chinese soil, seldom got the priority it deserved during the famines, floods, revolts, revolutions and invasions in the first half of the 20th century. Amid all the injustice and inequality on every side, the churches, believers, and missionaries had their hands full just staying alive.

This is not to judge nor excuse the actions of those pioneer foreign missionaries and Chinese Christians who seldom saw a time of peace. It was as if they were trying to plant rice and cotton during a continual typhoon. Any crop at all is a miracle.

World War II ended in 1945 and many missionaries returned to China to take up where they had left off in 1939 or 1941. I recall talking with a number of Presbyterians in Taiwan about those years. The Taiwanese church is in the main a Presbyterian church. One night in 1959 I was visiting with some of the Taiwanese Christians. They had all grown up in Presbyterian churches in southern Taiwan.

"When Japan bombed Pearl Harbor in 1941," one of the men began, "the missionaries from America, Canada and England left for the most part." Taiwan was at that time, and had been since 1895, a colony of Japan.

"Before they left," he went on, "They signed over all the mission and church-owned property to the Taiwanese Christian leaders or Presbyterian church of Taiwan."

His friend then added, "When they came back after the defeat of Japan they came not as supervisors but servants of the Taiwanese church. They came back to a church that had suffered and carried on without them."

The Taiwanese had learned how to lead. The locals knew now they could reach their own people as well, if not better, than the foreigner. So they welcomed the missionaries back, as it were "under new management," as equals, not overseers.

This did not represent the view of all Taiwanese believers any more than it represented the view of all the missionaries. Some were shocked to come back to "their work" and find they were not as needed (in the same way) as before.

Others rejoiced with the Taiwanese in their growth and maturity. There had been, during the war with Japan, a great revival among the mountain peoples of Taiwan. Much of this was as a result of the Taiwanese Christians reaching out to their aborigine brothers in their time of need. This unusual moving of the Spirit of God planted the seeds of indigenization that the churches of Taiwan needed.

After World War II, unlike World War I, the western powers returned to China what Japan had taken from them. Taiwan was returned to Chinese rule for the first time in fifty years.

By the time 1949 dawned it had become evident that the Republic of China under the Nationalists leadership could not bring China through the troubles that beset them on all sides. President Chiang Kai-shek (Jiang Jieshi) took his government and armed forces to Taiwan where he had already installed a military governor.

The Communist Party under the leadership of Mao Zedong, won the Civil War and proclaimed a new government, the People's Republic of China, on October 1, 1949 in Beijing (Peking, but called Pei P'ing by the Nationalists).

The missionaries, by and large, favored the Nationalists. The American press, led by *Time* and *Life* magazines, pictured the Nationalists' cause as the Christian answer for China. Henry Luce, the founder of *Time* and *Life*, was the son of missionaries who began Presbyterian work in Penglai in 1897 and had helped to build Yanjing University in Beijing. Three of the four leading Nationalists families were believed to be dedicated Christians. Many American Christian publications, and Luce's magazines, made the Communists into Public Enemy Number One.

The missionaries began to leave China. In June 1950 the Korean War broke out. After the threat of the American General Douglas MacArthur (1880-1964) to invade China, (he wanted to use Chiang Kai-shek's forces on Taiwan), most American missionaries in China went to other Asian countries to work or retired.

Southern Baptist's only fatality was the death in prison of Dr. William Wallace who served some 15 years as a missionary doctor in the Stout Memorial Baptist Hospital in the city of

Wuzhou in Guangxi province. Dr. Wallace chose to stay on rather than leave when the other missionaries did. On my first visit to Hong Kong in May, 1957, I met Bill Wallace's servant and helper. He took the doctor his meals while he was in prison. He was a gracious and good helper even to the end. He and other co-workers of Bill Wallace attest to the fact that Bill was not a spy as he was accused by the local authorities. It was a simple case of injustice. Injustice that grew out of a lack of understanding of the Christian faith as we know it. But not as the Chinese viewed Christianity.

Many Christians had let the world know their fear and hatred of communism. Many communists accepted these attitudes as valid expressions of Christ and Christianity. In such ignorance, Dr. Bill Wallace, China's friend, became the enemy to the new local officials, men with little knowledge of the Christ Wallace served. They were only aware that Wallace was an American and China was fighting Americans in Korea.

In December 1984 Cornellia Leavell (who was born of missionary parents in Wuzhou and knew Bill Wallace when she was a missionary kid in Wuzhou, then pronounced something like "Woo Chau"), Betty Vaught, and Bob Davis, went from Hong Kong to Wuzhou to reclaim the remains of Bill Wallace. A moving memorial scene was held in Wallace's home town in Tennessee the next month. Another evidence that *reasonable* Communist leaders in China are as concerned as any people to right wrongs and find ways for mutual understanding. There are just not enough *reasonable* Communist leaders.

From 1950 to 1960 Christians in China were seeking to find how to relate to the new situations. It was a road no one had ever walked before. It was a road the Chinese believer must learn to walk with the other Chinese, for all were wrapped up in the bundle of life, all were facing an uncertain future.

At the Yanjing School of Religion in Beijing, Professor T. C. Chao (Zhao Zichen, 1888-1979), was much involved in the changing times. He saw a challenge for Christians to become more aware of their heritage and concerned for their future. He was unsure about communism but open to what would help China. Chao, Y. T. Wu (Wu Yaozong 1893-1979) and other church leaders met with Premier Zhou Enlai to try and find out what role, if any, Christianity might play in China's future. Chao was also one of the initiators of "The Christian Manifesto," of 1950.

Y. T. Wu, a prime leader in the Three-Self Movement, writing in 1950-52, tried to help Christians appreciate the true meaning of God's omnipresence. Too many Christians, he wrote, "are bewildered because they refuse to see God's light which comes through unexpected channels." To Wu, the Communist Party was one such channel. He was accused of being a Communist, even falsely charged as identifying the accomplishments of the New China with the advent of the Kingdom of God. He never even implied such. Wu said he "believed that communism could be the vehicle for human betterment and that Christians could learn from people, even atheists."

Much of the struggle that Christians went through in the early years of the People's Republic of China was determined by their particular denominational or theological heritage. There had always been in many China churches the desire to be separate from the world, from worldly influences. Many felt they must even withdraw from family or friends who were not believers. Some took the apostle John to an extreme when he spoke of "Love not the world, neither the things that are in the world." This drawing apart for the Chinese Christians was no more helpful than the monks of the Middle Ages to hide in caves. Being "apart" did not make for spiritual development nor present a good witness to their unbelieving countrymen.

Until his death in January 1989 my friend John M. K. Jiang was pastor of the Huxi Church of Shanghai. On one of my last visits with him he shared the following with me:

"I had the experience of conversion and accepted Jesus Christ as my Savior at the age of 16. From that time on the only aim of my life has been to live for Jesus and serve him. Jesus became the center of my life. But I am sorry to say I went to an extreme position. I wrongly considered if Jesus were the center of my life I should isolate myself from the outer world. In other words, to me spirituality came to mean isolation. So during my four years of study at St. John's University in Shanghai, I didn't step into the University Christian Fellowship even once! I thought them too worldly.

"I had the same experience as Peter. I thought them 'not kosher.' Peter lagged behind God's eternal plan that included everybody. Thank God Peter changed and so have I. I shall never make the mistake of isolating myself from all the people again."

This was the tradition of many China Christians. They followed what they had been taught and continued to build walls around their faith instead of building bridges to their own people. Many had become so isolated they did not know what was going on in their own society.

The other extreme is equally dangerous. While being with unbelievers we must not forget the Apostle Paul's words that "All things are lawful but not all things are expedient" isolates in another way. Social and political involvement are vital to ministry but not at the expense of spiritual development. Social ministry only succeeds when driven by a spiritual motor. A good motor only runs smooth when all parts are properly balanced as the engineer planned it.

The People's Republic of China was still forming when the Korean War made the United States a very visible enemy. Many of the China churches were begun by American missionaries. The KMT (or Nationalists, *Guomingdang*) leaders were known to be Christian and very pro-American. The communists began to put pressure on anyone with American connections to stand up and be counted for the New China. In some areas former missionary co-workers were denounced. This was a political move and not a religious one. Robert T. Bryan, an American lawyer, living and working in Shanghai, and son of Southern Baptist missionaries, was jailed during this time. The thrust was against America more than against Christianity. This is another reason Christianity in China needs Chinese rather than foreign roots.

Through the Three-Self Movement Chinese Christians could separate themselves from their missionary past and seek to work more closely with their own people and aims of the New China.

This did not make them Communists any more than to become a Baptist in Texas means you have to become a Republican.

By 1957-58 churches in the major cities were being united. Shanghai, with more churches than any city in China, soon had only one church in a district, rather than dozens of denominational churches. From all the people I have talked to across China most explain it like one pastor: "None of our churches in those days were anywhere near full. By coming together we had a feeling of strength. That we were a minority was true, but we did not feel so alone in larger worship gatherings." Not everyone liked this nor cooperated. Especially those who had let their church become a society unto itself, forgetting that the church is not to become a separate society, but to serve in society.

In 1957 Chen Zemin (we met him in Chapter One) wrote a paper entitled: "The Task of Theological Construction in the Chinese Church." Here are excerpts of that essay. As you read this remember it was written over 40 years ago, in the midst of great uncertainty for Christianity in China.

"Our experience and understanding, although fragmentary and incomplete, are yet neither chaotic nor isolated. We are in a turbulent era, a society brimming with creative power, a period of rapid historical advance, and many things are progressing by leaps and bounds. Due to the sluggishness of our faith and the cloudiness of our vision, however, our understanding frequently lags behind reality. The revelation of God shows itself in earthquake and in fire, but in our weakness, we cover our ears and hide our eyes; we dare not face it. But we can in no way escape the advance of the torrent. Our faith is merely sluggish -- it has not died; our eyes are cloudy--but we have not grown blind. In the mighty streams of history, we are pushed forward by an irresistible force, and from among the many shattered whirlpools and spray flying in all directions, we can discern the path of the main current. If we examine the crumbs scattered on the floor, we shall see the loving face of the Giver of Life when we have filled 12 baskets with them. Spiritual hunger urges us to grope forward, and the path we follow is but the finger of God leading us."

The narrow view that a Christian living happily in a socialist society cannot be a real believer is just not true. That old bucket has never held water. It is too narrow a view even for Jesus, who was constantly trying to help his Jewish disciples see the good in their cousins across the way, the Samaritans.

Many good religious Jews could not believe that "love your neighbor" could include the Romans with their foreign ways and government.

Huang Peixin writing in the July 1957 issue of the *Nanjing Seminary Journal* (pages 8-10) points out that becoming a Christian is receiving a new life in Christ which does not link one with any particular social system.

With these two extremes (on the right the isolationists or "be ye separate" emphasis, and on the left those putting less emphasis on religion and the Bible and more on politics) a few men tried to bring some unity to the Christian scene. The attempt for unity came to be known as the Three-Self Patriotic Movement. The Three-Self principle being that of self-government, self-support and self-propagation.

In the working out of this principal it has come to be expressed in Chinese as *aijiao aiguo* (love the church and love the motherland).

With such an emphasis the Three-Self Movement was trying to bridge the gap between believers as well as with the nation as a whole. This was not an automatic result of the communist victory and new government. The primary question after the government was formed was, "Will there be freedom of religion in China under the leadership of the Communist Party? Will it be possible for the church to continue to exist?" These were the questions uppermost in the minds of most Chinese Christians in 1949-51.

Y. T. Wu and other Christian leaders began promotion of the Three-Self ideal in the early 1950s. This grew out of desires even as early as October 1949 for a nationwide meeting of Protestants. At such a meeting it was hoped to discuss China's new situation and what the Christian's response should be.

This was widely circulated beginning with the October 22, 1949 issue of *Tian Feng*. These early attempts to meet and talk over the problems and challenges of the future came to nothing. With a continued emphasis on mutual respect among believers and toward the government Y.T. Wu was finally able to get 232 representatives from 62 churches and Christian organizations to Beijing for the First National Christian Conference.

This historic gathering met from July 22 to August 6. Never before had this many Christians from such diverse backgrounds met on one platform. For this was not simply a time of tea and fellowship but a time for finding how they could work together and learn the lessons of "mutual respect" in a more meaningful way. This meeting was almost the exact opposite of the meeting in Shanghai at the turn of the Century when the 100th anniversary of Christian missions was celebrated. At that meeting no Chinese leaders had an active leadership part; it was a foreign missionary gathering. In 1950, half a century later, there were no missionaries and the Chinese were in the leadership position.

They had to find ways to work with the New China government that did not compromise the Christian's faith. Finding the best road to take took far more courage than to stand outside and refuse to go in like the elder brother in Jesus' parable in the New Testament (Luke 15:25-31).

Philip Wickeri, author of *Seeking the Common Ground*, relates what K. H. Ting said in 1949: "Upon entering the new situation of Communist control, if we must err, I would prefer to err on the side of naiveté rather than cynicism. The cynic bangs the door of opportunity himself and lands himself in nothing but spiritual frustration and greater cynicism. But the naive Christian worker sticks to his job. Doors banged against him will eventually give him the needed corrective to make him a true realist. There seem to be some redeeming possibilities in naiveté which cynicism lacks."

Dr. Wickeri goes on to say, "Christians who commit themselves to social movements have tended more towards the innocence of the dove than they have towards the wisdom of the serpent. ... But, as K. H. Ting reminds us, there is a sense of hopefulness and openness to the future which can redeem naive innocence and put it on firmer footing."

In May, 1950, before the First Christian Conference, a delegation of nineteen church leaders met with Premier Zhou Enlai in Beijing. Their report was to show what the Christian situation was and how it could relate to the New China. Premier Zhou Enlai's knowledge of Christianity in China was probably more than most of the government leaders at the time. That is an impression, not a fact. Zhou Enlai even remarked of knowing Christians when he was a student at Nankai Middle School in Tianjin. He found no problem with Christianity. The focus of attention was to see that foreign domination or foreign mission forces no longer have the former ties.

The group of nineteen followed up this meeting with the first drafts of a "Christian Manifesto". It is evident from a reading of the document that it was as much for the foreign "imperialists" as for local consumption.

The Christians struggled with the "Manifesto" mainly from the fact that as a whole they had not seen Christianity or the foreign missionary endeavor as closely linked with imperialism as had their government and some church leaders. Especially in the countryside, where most of China's churches and Christians were, there was little knowledge of mission history. All they knew was their own experience of salvation and grace. The church was a place for retreat, for worship, a time to be near God. It was this and nothing more for most of China's believers.

Christians would come into the New China much as the masses did, with fear and trembling. Rumors always seem to carry more weight than facts. And the land was rife with rumors of what the Communist would do to the people. In some places it was bad. There was unnecessary slaughter and intimidation. The excesses of revolution cannot be justified. They just are.

Wang Zizong, a Congregationalist leader from North China tried to clarify political implications in the "Manifesto." He wrote that "As Christians we should not say that all politics is of the devil, for such an attitude is just other-worldly and escapist. Nor should we say that any political system is entirely of God, for this smacks of confusing one thing for another and is not in the Christian spirit. The spirit of the genuine Christian is to act according to the blessings, intelligence and experience bestowed on us by God and do what is required by the age in which we live. God is the final authority for whatever success or failure we encounter. We can do no more than follow where he leads us doing what we should do in this age."

The Christian Manifesto, officially titled: "The Direction of Endeavor for Chinese Christianity in the Construction of New China" (*Zhongguo Jidujiao zai xin Zhongguo jianshe zhong nuli de tujing*), appeared in the August 19, 1950 issue of *Tian Feng*.

Y.T. Wu and forty leaders proclaimed this Christian Manifesto on July 28, 1950. The announcement was to initiate the Christian movement of reform. This was reported in full in *Tian Feng*, May 8, 1951.

A lot of new problems faced these leaders as they tried to practice the policy of mutual respect. It was one thing to say you believed such a thing, quite another to work it out in your life-style and behavior. Not every Christian body or church joined in. Wang Mingdao (Wang Ming Tao), a gifted preacher and evangelist became the most outspoken against any Christians that would even dialogue with the government authorities.

Wang Mingdao's church in Beijing was not linked to any foreign missionary heritage nor was it part of a Chinese denomination. He was an outstanding evangelist of the 1930s and 1940s following in the train of such men as John Sung (Song Shangjie, 1901-1944) and Leland Wang. Wang Mingdao would not acknowledge the Japanese when they were in control of north China, nor would he accept the leadership of the Communist Party for his motherland.

There developed a war of words between Wang Mingdao and the Three-Self Movement Committee. Both sides going beyond the bounds of Christian charity. The Three-Self leadership erred during these years in trying to force unity on the churches that they knew would keep the government off their backs. The idea was not to form a government-controlled church but one that could continue even under communism. They knew what had happened in Russia.

Wang Mingdao was very anti-Three-Self and adhered to Second Corinthians 6:14, "Be ye not unequally yoked together with unbelievers." He saw the Three-Self Movement not only as unchristian, but plotting actively against the churches.

This unwillingness to find ways to work with other Christians brought forth an article by K. H. Ting. It reads in part:

"The Holy Spirit is testing our love to see whether or not we are really servants of God ... Mutual respect not only requires us to see that others respect us, it also calls us to learn humility, the love of others and the value of other persons, and to see the other's good points.

"Learning to respect others means that we must acknowledge that they have points which are worthy of respect. It means that we must learn to see other people as Jesus saw them. If we are proud and arrogant, if we consider everyone and everything unworthy of our attention, if we reject another's faith as wretched, then we do not know how to respect others. Paul wanted us to 'do nothing from selfishness or conceit, but in humility count others better than ourselves.' (Philippians 2:3) When others reviled him or leveled irresponsible criticism at him, Paul said, 'Look at what is before your eyes. If one is confident that he is Christ's, let him remind himself that as he is Christ's, so are we.'"

The founder-leader of the *Jidutu Juhuichu* or Christian Assembly (more widely known in English as "The Little Flock"), was Watchman Nee (Ni Duosheng). Nee is more widely known in the English-speaking world than in China. He wanted indigenous churches. Soon the Little Flock had become a denomination of its own. Founded in 1922 about the time of the True Jesus Church (1917) and the Jesus Family (1921) "Little Flock" led the way in being "apart" from the world, including other fundamentalists.

The True Jesus Church was founded by Paul Wei in Beijing May 1, 1917. *Tian Feng* reported in the February 23, 1952, edition that Paul Wei's son Isaac reported 1000 churches and 100,000 members still active in the early 1950s.

Problems from the "leftist" side of the picture that opposed Three-Self were those who should be called "ultra-leftist." They saw salvation more in the pursuit of patriotic and political goals rather than in biblical theology and Christian practice. These neglected the sheep while trying to please the Communist Party, come what may.

It is easy, but dangerous, to sit in judgment of history. As has been said, we are too removed from the original experience to fully appreciate it all. We tend in the research of history to pick and choose. This can leave the story only partially told and not completely understood.

The Second National Christian Conference was held in Shanghai from November 12, 1960 until January 14, 1961. There were 319 delegates from 25 provinces. This was only a few years before the so-called Cultural Revolution would break forth all over China and destroy much of what good had been accomplished. This was the last such conference for twenty years.

The Third National Christian Conference was held in Shanghai in October 1980. The urgency of opening the churches and getting theological education going again was uppermost in this meeting.

The Fourth National Christian Conference was held in Beijing, August 16-23, 1986. All regions, except Tibet, were represented. Many more lay people attended and at least a third of the delegates were women. Each of the seminaries were represented with faculty and students.

The Fifth National Conference was held in October, 1992.

To understand the 1950s in China more of the history and development of the Three-Self Movement needs to be studied rather than written off as just another good or bad movement. What they struggled and worked over during those years is bearing fruit today all over China. They made mistakes. Everyone does, unless they do nothing. These men could not "do nothing," they had to ensure the gospel would continue to be preached and shared in China. Only this time it had to be the planting of local seeds in order to grow local churches filled with Chinese Christians.

They were taking the promise to Judah in the Old Testament that their work would "take root downward and bear fruit upward" (Isaiah 37:31). This promise recorded centuries ago has become as applicable to the China of today as to it was to the Judah of old.

CHAPTER FOUR

The Years of the Locust, 1966-1976
The "Cultural Revolution" Years

"Why do you say, 'My way is hidden from the Lord, and the justice due me escapes the notice of my God?' Do you not know? Have you not heard? The Everlasting God, the Lord, the creator of the ends of the earth does not become weary or tired. His understanding-is inscrutable. He gives strength to the weary, and to him who lacks might He increases power... Those who wait for the Lord will gain new strength; They will mount up with wings like eagles, They will run and not get tired, They will walk and not become weary."
--Isaiah 40:27-31

No darker days ever crossed China's horizon than those that began forming in the early 1960s when Jiang Qing, wife of China's leader Mao Zedong, took control of Mao's "purge" of the Communist Party and began planting seeds for what came to be known as "The Great Proletarian Cultural Revolution" -- a movement that history has proven had absolutely nothing to do with culture or revolution.

It was an excuse to turn the youth of China loose to do anything they cared to do in eradicating the "Four Olds." Christianity and religion were considered a part of the old ideas, culture, customs and habits that had to go. Christianity had the added problem of being considered foreign, so it was evil on two counts -- religion was bad enough, but a foreign religion definitely had no place in the Red Guard's New China.

On August 8, 1966, the Chinese Communist Party Central Committee adopted the "Decision concerning the Great Proletarian Cultural Revolution." Typical of the frenzy of those

39

days was a poster put up at the entrance of the former YMCA building in Beijing. It read:

> There is no God; there is no Spirit; there is no Jesus; there is no Mary; there is no Joseph. How can adults believe in these things? ... Priests live in luxury and suck the blood of the workers. ... Like Islam and Catholicism, Protestantism is a reactionary feudal ideology, the opium of the people, with foreign origins and contacts. ... We are atheists; we believe only in Mao Zedong. We call on all people to burn bibles, destroy images and disperse religious associations. (Philip L. Wickeri. *Seeking the Common Ground*, New York: Orbis Books, 1988, p. 180)

Temples and monasteries, churches and cathedrals, schools of all descriptions came in for tremendous desecration and defacing. Had not Premier Zhou Enlai intervened, the Confucian temples in Shandong Province -- where Confucius was born and lived -- would have been totally leveled. He could not save everyone and everything, but he was one of the few in a position of power who gave glimmers of light and sanity during these years.

As the churches were closed to worship, they began to be used for everything from factories and storehouses to local headquarters for the rampaging Red Guards, the young people turned loose to purge the land and people and make a new China.

Years later, a lovely Christian lady in Shanghai shared what it was like to be shut out of her church building during those years. With tears, she remembered the Christmas seasons of those unreal years of the "Cultural Revolution". She said they would walk down to the church building well after dark. Not being able to enter the gate and courtyard, they would just walk around the walls and find solace in being near God's house at that season-- walking and remembering the former days, the days when they could go inside and worship the Savior. As she shared this with me in the back of a packed Shanghai church in

1983, she could not finish the story. For memories of sadness mixed with the present joy of being again in God's house was much too overwhelming.

She had only begun to share a little with me because I understood the language. She had not planned to say so much. The joy of being free to worship again and to come into the house of the Lord and talk to a fellow-Christian from afar got the best of her emotions. This has been our experience all over China. The Christians say little of past hardships and misfortunes. They do not dwell on the past. For some it is a horror they never care to recall -- for others an experience of grace too personal and private to speak about. What they do radiate now is the presence of the Lord who went with them through the valley of the shadow.

The swarthy young guards would enter the churches like a conquering army. They could roam at will and feel that what they destroyed was good for China. Once such destructive forces were unleashed, they became as a great tidal wave sweeping away everything in its path.

In a southern city, after romping recklessly through the church building and transforming the house of prayer into a literal house of waste, human and otherwise, the Red Guards, *hongweibing*, turned their attention to the pastor and his family. First they ordered the pastor and members of his family to carry all the Bibles and hymn books out of the church and into the street. There the Christians were forced, on their knees, to burn the Bibles and hymnals, page by page.

Since the pastor and his family lived in the rear of the church, they had to move out. It would be a long time before that church building would be useful for anything. Christian friends were careful in lending a helping hand to the pastor and his family lest they should get the same treatment. This Christian pastor was wrong -- had wasted his life and time -- and anyone found helping him would be in the same boat! This was the message of the Red Guards to that town. This was the way of the extremist, the ultra-leftist.

As tempers cooled in the area, the pastor was able to get a job in a local factory. His wife began doing sewing and handwork -- hardly the kind of labor that would earn enough money to buy food. Though forbidden to speak of Christ, the pastor found he could witness better than before. His life was his testimony. His attitude was his sermon. He was different, and the difference spoke of a strength and grace that so many in the factory were seeking. It was evident that the Holy Spirit was in his new work. He understood the hurt and humiliation of his people. The cold written doctrine of God's grace and presence had become a warm, vibrant and living experience.

In the north central China city of Kaifeng, a Christian lady well-known in the community for her active church life and love of the Savior was led through the streets, hands tied behind her, a cardboard sign around her neck denouncing her as a believer in a foreign religion. Among the crowd that day stood a former powerful city leader, now helpless to do anything but watch. He watched her face, observed her attitude, and studied her expression as she was subjected to such strain. It was unlike anything he had ever seen before.

Years later when the land had returned to some normality, he sought out the woman he was told was Wang Delu. He said to her, "I have come because I want to know the God you know -- the one I saw on your face that day in the street." Wang Delu and many like her witnessed the only way they could -- in silence and turning the other cheek. When I met her some years later she was all I had heard her to be. Later Christian friends made it possible for her to visit the United States and share her testimony with a number of churches.

Wang Delu was a colleague with Southern Baptist missionaries Maude and Wilson Fielder and others in Henan province before the majority of foreign missionaries were forced to leave China in 1949 and 1950.

I remember visiting with a lovely lady in Hong Kong in 1967. She had just been to see her husband in China. She and the children had left China six years earlier and settled in Hong Kong, hoping he would be able to join them soon. He had waited too long to seek the exit permit, and it now appeared impossible for him to rejoin his family.

She told me of her most recent trip.

42

"Do you have your Bible still?" she asked her husband as soon as they were safely inside his small one-room apartment.

Quietly he moved to the little pile of firewood in the corner. From beneath the sticks he pulled his worn Bible. When his wife wanted to read from it and pray aloud, her husband warned her against it.

"One never knows who is listening these days," he cautioned her. "This is not the China you and the children left six years ago. The neighbors might report us to the authorities. The last thing we need around here are those ranting young kids, the ones who call themselves Red Guards."

So each day the couple read and prayed silently. But after a week of this restraint, his wife -- so influenced by years in Hong Kong churches -- felt she must sing praises to God, and aloud. However, in those moments of weakness she also recognized the wisdom of not doing so.

In the hope of being alone, the reunited couple went for a walk one afternoon, but even in the park near his apartment they could not get away from people. Privacy had always been rare in China, but not to the extent, she felt, of these days of upheaval. There seemed to be no place in the land anymore where believers could open their mouths to sing and praise God.

Then the rain began -- falling slowly at first and finally coming down in torrents. This is the limit, she thought. Even when we try to get out and forget our troubles, we are forced inside again by the weather.

No sooner had the thought crossed her mind than she began to regret it. In delighted amazement she and her husband looked about them. The rain had turned the park into a deserted place.

Everyone had fled to shelter. They were alone -- soaked, but alone! In the downpour the two held hands as they began to sing an old favorite hymn they had memorized long ago:

> Amid the trials that I meet,
> Amid the thorns that pierce my feet,
> One thought remains supremely sweet:
> Thou thinkest, Lord, of me.

43

The cares of life come thronging fast,
Upon my soul their shadows cast;
Their gloom reminds my heart at last,
Thou thinkest, Lord, of me.

Let shadows come, let shadows go,
Let life be bright or dark with woe;
I am content, for this I know,
Thou thinkest, Lord, of me.

The comfort of God's eternal abiding care and concern filled their souls. They looked at each other and then to the sky. A bright rainbow crossed the heavens, seeming to shout God's pleasure with them in his acceptance of their worship. I wrote this story first for *The Commission Magazine*, November, 1967.

Professor Yang, who taught math in a Shanghai university, was put in a Shanghai jail because he was caught listening to western classical music on his phonograph. The "Cultural Revolution" years were truly the years in which the locust feasted. Common sense went out the window.

As I was getting a haircut in the capital of Henan province, the conversation came around to those terrible years. I commented to the barber that such tragic years as those of the "Cultural Revolution" must never come again to China. The barber agreed. Then he stopped cutting my hair and came around to look me in the face. He said, almost in anger, "It is all well and good that there must never again be such a waste, but what about me? My schooling was not only interrupted, but stopped after the fourth grade. My family was ruined. You can't go back and change that!"

They have been called the lost generation. They lost out when schools were closed, when neighbors were suspect, when classical music was unfit for the Chinese ear.

Churches and Christians were not the only ones to suffer during these years. I have been honored to meet numbers of musicians, writers, teachers and intellectuals of all persuasions who were made to kneel in the streets -- dunce caps upon their heads -- to be maligned by the taunting Red Guards day without

44

end. All of China suffered through days and years that seemed to have no end in sight.

For the Chinese, death is more often to be desired than humiliation. A great many men and women -- Christian and non-Christian -- chose death rather than such degradation. Shu Qingchun, better known as Lao She, one of the greatest writers of the twentieth century in China is an example of preferring death to the ignorant harassment of the empty-headed and senseless attacks of Mao's young people gone crazy.

Lao She's son, Shu Yi, in a 12-part series about his father, wrote of the night his father could take no more of the madness. It was August 23 as he left his office in the cultural affairs building in Beijing when the Red Guards seized him and began berating him. They put a sign around his neck, spit on him and cursed him merely for being an intellectual who had taught in England and visited America. All that made him the enemy.

His wife found him later and got him home. But the next morning, with little rest, he set off for his office. Just before going out the door he called his three-year-old granddaughter to him, and holding her tightly by the hand, he said, "Tell Granddaddy good--bye--!" He left the house and walked out. He went to a small lake a good ways from his home. There he must have considered the unreal treatment he had received the night before.

Later when I came to know Lao She's son, Shu Yi, he told me "We have no idea how long he sat beside the small Taiping Lake in Beijing's western suburbs, nor what he was thinking there in the moonlight. He was a man of character and could not accept the lies of the Red Guards, to whom he was a disgrace; nor that his writings were just a putrid mess."

Lao She, who gave the Chinese and the world their best insight into Old Beijing life in his writings, was now an outcast in his own beloved city. His book *Luotuo Xiangzi*, better known to the Western world as *Rickshaw Boy*, the title used in two film versions, made old Beijing come alive to millions who never saw the ancient capital. His three-act play, *Teahouse*, was a unique way to show fifty years of modern Chinese history set simply in a Beijing teahouse.

Sometime that night or in the early morning hours, Lao She walked away from such humiliation into the Taiping Lake. He would not compromise with such young fools. Life had no meaning if such were to be the final word, the law of China.

There are a number of scholars who feel Lao She was murdered by the Red Guards that night. We will never know, but it is certain the Red Guards reckless actions led to his death. Regardless of how he died, he would not compromise with such young thugs in the name of progress.

Rev. Li Ke, one of the pastors of the Gangwashi Church in Beijing, shared with me that Lao She had been a Christian since the early 1920s and had taught Sunday school in the Gangwashi Church at one time. For more on Lao She see my book, *Lao She, China's Master Storyteller*. (Waco: Tao Foundation, 1999).

The year before he died, Lao She wrote a brief poem he called "My Present." Here is the way Rewi Alley (1897-1987) translated it into English. It was originally published in 1977 in the *Renmin wen xue*:

> Late in life, but happiness surrounds,
> No worries whatever to bow me down;
> My children competing in their work,
> Workers and peasants all joining together.
> Poems sing of the new,
> The pen rids itself of old styles.
> Don't laugh at my walking stick!
> I will always march forward with head held high.

Deng Pufang, the son of China's greatest revolutionary, Deng Xiaoping (who will more likely be remembered for his actions against the students in Tiananmen Square in 1989), was a student at Beijing University when the "Cultural Revolution" erupted. Deng Pufang was grabbed and thrown by the Red Guards from an upstairs window of his dorm simply because he was the son of a man who saw some good in the "capitalists' road." Some say he fell trying to escape the Red Guards, regardless he lives out his life in a wheelchair, never to walk again.

Even heroes who had traveled with Mao Zedong on the Long March suffered during the "Cultural Revolution." The Long March began in on the border of Jiangxi and Fujian provinces October 16, 1934 with 86,000 troops. The 6,000 mile trek to escape the Nationalists ended October 19, 1935, in Yan'an, northern Shaanxi province, with only 4,000 soldiers. Those who suffered through the Long March and then were purged in the "Cultural Revolution" included the PRC President Liu Shaoqi (left to die untreated in Kaifeng November 12, 1969); Peng Dehuai, commander of the forces against the Japanese and later against the Americans in Korea (after eight years of abuse died November 29, 1974); Zhu De, founder of the Red Army (shamelessly mistreated; even his wife Kang Keqing was made to parade through the streets as a traitor. Zhu De died in July 1976).

The West knew nothing of the Communist Long March until Edgar Snow visited Yan'an in 1936 and wrote about the historic march and the Communist leaders in his book *Red Star Over China*.

The "Cultural Revolution" was not primarily a time of religious persecution. Dr. Philip L. Wickeri, who is writing a biography of the paramount leader of Protestants in China, Bishop K. H. Ting, expressed the attitude of Chinese Christians and persecution best when he wrote: "Chinese Christians have not emphasized their own special suffering during the decade which is now termed a ten year disaster, for to do so would undermine the solidarity which they have gained with the rest of the Chinese people. During the 'Cultural Revolution' Christians suffered *with* the Chinese people, not *for* them."

Having suffered together they know better how to minister to one another and how to relate the message of Christ to their own people in a way few foreigners or outsiders can fully appreciate.

Rev. Zheng Yugui of the Flower Lane Church in Fuzhou told of a member of his church that was sent away from her home and family during the "Cultural Revolution". Sent from her children and loved ones to a desolate forsaken place in the mountains, she became so depressed with the surroundings and difficult work that she wanted to jump from one of the high cliffs and end her life. But each time this temptation would come to her a verse from the Bible would come back to her mind and heart: "Though I walk through the valley of the shadow of death, I will fear no evil, for Thou art with me; Thy rod and Thy staff they comfort me." When this verse came to her heart she no longer thought of death for God was with her. He had not left her alone. After those troubled years she was able to return home again and is today an active member of the Fuzhou church.

Thousands of Christians and non-Christians alike lived through a darkness of fear and uncertainty that took its toll on all. Among them were those who knew the reality of what the poet Longfellow meant when he wrote: "Know how sublime a thing it is to suffer and be strong."

A Bible verse that encouraged many in those "Cultural Revolution" days was Romans 8:18 -- "The sufferings of this present time are not worthy to be compared with the glory which shall be revealed in us."

It was a time to learn the meaning of much of the Bible's truths. Where two or three are gathered in the name of Jesus there was comfort, there was worship, there was fellowship.

Bishop K. H. Ting, of the Anglican tradition, retired principal of the Jinling Union Theological Seminary in Nanjing. He is the Past President of the National Three-Self Patriotic Movement and the China Christian Council. He told me: "Many of us found it spiritually sustaining and fulfilling meeting together in homes. Christians ministered to each other. It was a time to learn of the preciousness of the Bible, a time given to remembering and recovering passages of the Bible that were dear to us."

K. H. Ting studied as a young man at Columbia University and the Union Theological Seminary in New York City. He served for a time as secretary of the Student Christian Movement of Canada and later as a member of the World Student Christian Federation in Geneva, Switzerland. In addition to his seminary and church duties, he is presently a Vice President of Nanjing University and President of the Institute for Religious Studies of the same institution. He is a leading member of the Standing

Committee of the National People's Congress. The Congress represents all the people, not just the communists. I found Bishop Ting to be one of the most intelligent and gracious Christian gentlemen it has been my privilege to know.

Regarding the years that the Red Guards rampaged over China, Bishop Ting shared with me that "The 'Cultural Revolution' was anti-cultural and not at all revolutionary. The church in Laodicea was our experience. In order to do God's will we must go through trials. Our gold had to be refined. Our clothes had to be without stain. We needed balm for the eyes. The ultra-leftists tried to do to China what her outside enemies could not do. They turned old revolutionaries into counter-revolutionaries. They tried to prove they were more true than all the others. We had our Peters, our Judases, our Thomases, but more Christians stayed steadfast in their faith than failed."

I asked Bishop Ting what was the most precious lesson gleaned from the years when the locust has ravaged China.

"It is our strengthened faith in the risen Christ," he said. "Resurrection is the most descriptive word for our Chinese experience. We learned what it is to die and live again. We learned that the principles of redemption and sanctification are based on the resurrection. Since we suffered with our people, we now are better identified with them. As Paul said, 'We bear in our bodies the death of Jesus Christ.' We have learned that life does not depend on power or wealth but on the life of Jesus Christ. The joy of the resurrection is the lesson that we have learned in these decades."

At the first graduation ceremony of Jinling Union Theological Seminary since its reopening in 1981, K. H. Ting recalled that his own major when in university was civil engineering. Being a pastor in those days was a humble existence. It took much prayer for God to show him he was needed in the Christian ministry. Few at that June 29, 1985 ceremony knew that the then 70-year-old seminary principal who spoke to them of his early training in engineering had worked during part of the "Cultural Revolution" on building the great Nanjing Bridge that spans the mighty Yangtze River. His work there, though he was capable of greater things, was lowly and humble.

In the East China province of Zhejiang in the city of Hangzhou, Pastor Peter W. H. Tsai (Cai Wenhao), of the Presbyterian tradition, senior pastor of the Si Cheng Church, spoke of those years following the "Cultural Revolution": "Believers were very hungry and thirsty. For ten years they were not fed. When churches opened again, they were often lacking in many basic Bible doctrines. We would preach long sermons, fifty minutes or more. They would not like brief sermons. If we were to preach a brief sermon, they would scold us after the service. Every word was fresh to them."

Pastor Peter Tsai and his wife studied in the United States and suffered as did their co-workers and people during the "Cultural Revolution". He will not tell of being led through the streets of Hangzhou and other harsh treatment of those days, but he will smile and tell of God's goodness and mercy.

The locust destroyed a decade. The plague of the "Cultural Revolution" years was to become only a catalyst for a deeper faith and a greater China.

CHAPTER FIVE

The Years of Renewal, 1979-1989

Common Sense Makes A Comeback: Reopening of the Churches

"I am confident of this very thing, that He who began a good work in you will perfect it until the day of Christ Jesus."
--Philippians 1:6

On the day that Chairman Mao Zedong died, September 9, 1976, my youngest daughter and I were doing some shopping in the Central District of Hong Kong for the new school year. I looked up a few blocks to the Bank of China building and saw the huge Chinese words for "Chairman Mao" (*Mao zhuxi wansui* - "long live Chairman Mao") being lowered from the roof. I knew something had happened. It was such an abrupt, unexpected change -- and so sudden that it was difficult to believe he was really gone. Could anyone guess the changes that would continue to rock China right into the 21st century?

Within a month, Mao's widow Jiang Qing and her cohorts -- Zhang Chunqiao, who remained silent through his trial; Yao Wenyuan, who admitted his mistakes; and Wang Hongwen, who pleaded guilty -- were all arrested. Jiang Qing remained defiant throughout her arrest and trial. She died while serving a life sentence.

Only one church was known to have been opened during the "Cultural Revolution." On Easter Sunday, 1972, in Beijing Chinese-language services were held for foreign consulate personnel. This service was led by three Chinese pastors and an organist. They met in the former Bible Society house, number 21, Dongdan Bei Da Jie, in what was later known as the Mishi Tang or Rice Market Church. The church met there until the Congwenmen Church property could be reclaimed in 1982.

Beijing pastor Kan Xueqing told of the interest the United States President George Bush showed in Christian services when Bush was U.S. liaison officer to China. Pastor Kan said, "Even though we could not hold services for our own people during those years, we were glad to help out the foreigners. I think he helped a lot of people see that being a Christian was not a small thing." One of the Bush daughters was baptized during their stay in Beijing in the early 1970s.

Mishi Tang later became the first church reopened in the capital. I worshipped with them one Sunday in December 1982, just a few weeks before they moved to their present location in Chongwenmen District. After the church moved, the Mishi Tang property became the headquarters for the YMCA and the Beijing Christian Council.

I quietly interpreted the sermon to my colleagues on the trip. We sat at the back and heard a sermon that mentioned the second coming of Christ. A topic I had been told in Hong Kong was not permitted in China. Dr. Jimmy R. Allen, then head of SBC Radio and Television ministry and musician Buryl Red and layman Ralph Tacker were in Beijing to arrange for the SBC men's choir, The Centurymen, to tour China. It was also my first time to worship on the mainland.

But the first churches to re-open in 1979 were not in Beijing or Shanghai. It was in Ningbo, Zhejiang province, that the first Chinese-language church was reopened and services were held for the masses. It took a great deal of faith for the Bainian Church in Ningbo to take this step of open worship so soon after the members of the Gang of Four were arrested.

The Christians of Shanghai were asking for a place to worship and, finally, with the help of Sun Yanli, who had just retired from a factory in the spring of 1979, the prospects looked good for reclaiming the Muen Church on Xizang Zhong Road in the very center of Shanghai. Pastor Sun, a pastor at the Muen Church and principal of the East China (Huadong) Theological Seminary, recalled the summer of 1979: "We had no idea the government would listen to our requests. We just kept praying and submitting applications to regain what was rightfully ours under the constitution." Then, by midsummer, the Shanghai

Three-Self Committee was informed that it could reopen a church building for those Christians who might be interested in public worship. The authorities viewed such worship as a futile exercise in superstition.

"It was decided that the old Moore Memorial Methodist Church would be the easiest to renovate," continued Pastor (later Bishop) Sun. "The sanctuary had been used as a school auditorium. In the beginning we could use it only on Sundays. Huge portraits of Mao Zedong and Hua Guofeng were covered over with curtains each Sunday morning before the services could be held. People started lining up in the streets for the six a.m. first service every Sunday before four in the morning."

So in the very heart of one of the world's largest cities, after 13 years with no public worship, God reopened the doors of the former Moore Memorial Methodist Church, now the Muen Church. Three services each Sunday could not seat the people.

Muen Church's senior pastor at the time, the Rev. Shi Qigui, said it was the greatest experience of his life to actually see the doors open, to watch the people come in hours before the service to pray, weep and wait before the Lord. It was an event they had hardly dared dream about. Now it was happening. Here is how Shi Qigui described it to me in 1982:

"I was one of the younger pastors, only 50 years of age at the time, and my wife was still attached to a factory in another city, so I was both more able and free to help every Sunday morning to prepare the church for worship. The first months, the school continued to use the auditorium, and I would drape the portraits and get the chairs straight and everything in order. I usually had to begin at two in the morning, for the people began early to line up outside the gates. By four o'clock the sanctuary was filled. The first service began at 6:30. Two others followed, and we could not seat all the people. It was evident we needed more churches opened."

In the months and years to come, as churches opened, former Baptist Pastor Qi Qingcai was called on to preach the first sermon in the first four churches re-opened. The people loved this down-to-earth Shandong province preacher who loved the Lord and knew the Book well.

Six years later, October of 1985, the 22nd church in Shanghai was reopened. The 23rd church organized was Wusong near the mouth of the Yangzi River. Since one church has reverted to being a Meeting Point another church in the suburbs was organized as number 23 on June 5, 1988. How functioning churches revert to being Meeting Points is possibly due to lack of ordained leadership.

In addition to services in regular church-type buildings, thousands of Bible studies in homes (often referred to as "house churches" in the West) meet regularly. Some of these are sponsored by reopened churches. Others are a carry over from the "Cultural Revolution" days when home worship services and prayer times were all the people had.

In 1999, twenty years after the churches began to re-open, there are over 150 churches in the Shanghai area with over 150,000 members.

The July 1980 *National Geographic Magazine*, pages 8-9, has a striking photo by Bruce Dale of the Muen Church worship service during that first year. Pastor Shi Qigui is standing at the pulpit in the photo. It is wrongly captioned the "Mu An Church," but it is a collector's item of a photograph.

The Grace Church of Shanghai, formerly of the Baptist tradition, averages more than 5500 in three weekend services. When the church re-opened, Senior Pastor Qi Qingcai loved to tell, with beaming face and eyes aglow despite his 77 years, "We never had it like this before. Never have so many shown such interest in the Gospel of our Lord. We praise Him, for this is His doing, and His alone!" Pastor Qi served the church well until his death in February, 1990.

W.B. Glass, one of Southern Baptists' pioneer missionaries to Shandong province, was one of Qi Qingcai's teachers long ago in the Huangxian Baptist Boys Middle School. Dr. Glass, though a product of the 19th century missionary thrust, was one who saw the need of China's churches being Chinese -- to be supported, to be promoted, and to be developed by Chinese leadership. (For more on W. B. Glass see *Higher Ground* by Eloise Glass Cauthen, Broadman, 1978 and *Carey's China Jewell* by Britt Towery.)

Early this century, a visiting American Southern Baptist church leader was making a tour of the Southern Baptist mission fields. In those days the only Southern Baptist mission fields in Asia were China and Japan. I will never forget Dr. Glass telling us this story one night in Arizona. It went something like this:

The visiting American churchman spoke in one of the Shandong village churches, and Dr. Glass was his interpreter. The visitor, in his closing remarks to the church said, "You need a larger church building. When I get back to America and tell my church people about your situation, they will give you enough money to build a larger and nicer church."

Dr. Glass knew that none in the congregation understood a word of English, so he ably translated what the visitor *should* have said -- "I am so thankful for the work you are doing in this village, and thankful you have such a church that can be a beacon of light and hope to all in your village. I encourage you to keep on keeping on. We in America are praying for you."

The church grew in self-respect that night. The visitor was highly respected in their eyes thanks to the interpreter's wisdom. Many missionaries like W. B. Glass saw the real future of Christian ministry in China as belonging to the Chinese. The foreigner has been God's *meiren*, or "go-between," the one in Chinese tradition that helped young couples become acquainted and married. The missionary is to introduce the message, to bring the people to God, then get out of the way. The Holy Spirit does a better job in every culture working directly with the people of that culture.

The missionary must never look upon his ministry as a career in any country where he or she is a guest. The missionary is there to introduce Jesus to the people and then step behind the scenes, move to another village, or journey on to a new land. Financial subsidy and longtime direction from foreigners decreases the chances of the gospel taking root and flourishing in the local, native soil.

Pastor Qi Qingcai was honored by East Texas Baptist College (now university), Marshall, Texas, with an honorary degree in the late 1940s. When remembering his former missionary co-workers, he always came back to the present fact,

"The Lord's work has always been the most glorious work in the world; it is just that we have never seen it on this order before."

When the Grace Church property was cleared of former tenants (a factory that had been using the premises for more than 13 years) and they were allowed once again to enter and pray and worship, the church people got a local loan of 100,000 yuan (about US$35,000 at the time) to renovate and repair the church building. Within three years this loan had been repaid--entirely from the offerings of the people. Pastor Qi said: "I have never in my fifty years of ministry seen such dedication in giving as our people revealed and continue to reveal week after week."

I was tempted to ask how they could get 5500 people, on average, to the three services each weekend. He saw the question coming, and said, "We make all three of these weekly services identical as much as we can. This way we discourage our people from coming more than once a week to worship. Otherwise we would easily have over 10,000 in attendance each week."

"We are united," Qi added, "but that does not mean we are a union church in the way Baptists look at union." The churches of China had begun to unite in the mid-1950s. After the "Cultural Revolution," denominational differences did not mean all that much to the believers. Just to be able to worship was fulfilling. There was really no deep need to return to the former days of denominational bias in worship and fellowship. The Chinese Christians had all suffered together and now would worship together and unitedly share Christ with all of China and the world, as opportunity afforded itself.

The stressing of mutual respect and understanding has helped many who do feel a strong tendency to their own particular denominational tradition. The ordinances of baptism and the Lord's Supper are shared in any number of ways. Throughout Christian history, these have been debated and used as divisive doctrines, and so China today desires to let each congregation and each believer choose what is most natural to them and their faith.

Baptism is administered in various modes, with churches tending to follow the patterns of their own historical experience. The rite or mode of baptism is not what makes a man right with

God anyway; it merely indicates the road he now plans to walk with his new-found Lord and Savior.

Another leader, formerly of the Little Flock Fellowship, shared that he felt Christian churches in the rest of the world seemed to spend a lot of time on their differences. Those minute and minor things that keep denominations from each other, he said, should be avoided in the new China. "We do not want to have that sort of a future in our churches here in China," he said.

As Pastor Qi stated, unity is not necessarily union. Opinions differ on Biblical interpretation, on church polity, and on procedures, even within a single church -- just as they do in churches everywhere in the world. The unity is in the major doctrines of salvation, faith, hope and love. It is here that the churches of China can teach the rest of the world the true meaning of unity.

By 1989, a total of more than 6,375 churches had been reopened or newly built in China. In addition there were over 20,602 Meeting Points, of which over 15,000 actively cooperate with the China Christian Councils of their areas. Statistics are very difficult to obtain in such a large country with so many different ideas about the usefulness or necessity of such things. See the author's web site Mission Forum for photos of new China churches, Pastor Shi Qigui and Pastor Qi and wife and other China friends. (<www.laotao.org/mission>)

The term "house churches" came out of the "Cultural Revolution." It is not a new term but is as old as the New Testament, for in the Bible the only churches were "house churches" of one form or another. Christian places of worship had not evolved in those early days to what we know as church buildings in the 20th century. During the traumatic days of 1966-76, worship in homes -- if possible at all -- was all the believers had. Many new believers came to know the Lord in just such circumstances. It is only natural that many of these would want to stay with the only "church" they knew, the "house church." In those days they learned what it was to meet in silent worship, lest they be noticed or thought to be subversive. The educated and the peasant sat side by side and learned from each other.

K.H. Ting told me, "Our seminary became the headquarters of the Red Guards in Nanjing. We could not carry on as we had. We started meeting for tea to have prayer and read the Bible together. We found this kind of meeting very fulfilling. Through such sharing, our inner light became brighter. In such groups, each one was a minister, and each one was ministered to by the others.

"As a bishop I was not comfortable in such meetings, but I learned to be ministered unto. An important mark of Chinese Christianity is the small home meetings."

So it is that, with thousands of churches open, some believers still prefer to meet in homes. When Bishop K.H. Ting's mother was 97, she was still the leader of a home worship service. In July of 1986, at the age of one hundred, she went to be with the Lord.

For many Christians house meetings were all they knew of church or worship. Many knew little of formal church services in buildings. It is only natural that this form of worship would continue even when larger and more usable church buildings were available.

There are those Christians who are basically opposed to designated places of worship. These more independent groups of believers often tend to go out of their way to show that they are different. This has caused problems for them and the national church leadership. Some Christians outside of China, especially in Hong Kong, have interpreted this to mean that the Christians worshipping in homes more truly represent the "true church" -- as opposed to the open church that meets in public church buildings. Such a conclusion is arrived at only through guesswork, theological bias, and total distrust of the Three-Self motives and leadership. Such a view is out of touch with the reality of the social and religious situation in China today.

There is not a great diversity of opinion inside China itself, however, concerning home congregations, meeting points or house churches and churches that meet in what "looks-like" a church building. This is not one of the major problems facing the Christians of today's China. It is made to seem so by many of the research houses and organizations intent on turning back the clock and reintroducing denominational missions -- and once again putting the foreigner, whether overseas Chinese or Anglo, in charge of the emerging churches of China. The more I visited the churches of China and talk with the people and pastors of that great land, the more it became evident that the headquarters of the dissident house church is not in China but in Hong Kong and the United States. Home assembly points and open churches work hand in glove in most areas of China. The exception should not be made the rule.

For some, denominational ties held a little spiritual security, and they felt comfortable in a certain style of worship and church activity. There is nothing wrong in such sentiments. It is natural to remember one's spiritual roots. The Three-Self Movement of the 1950s was admittedly too abrupt in its attempts to achieve church unity. All of China was caught up in the sudden events and problems that came with the founding of the People's Republic of China on October 1, 1949. Then, just a few scant years later, this new nation was at war with the United States in Korea. America was the enemy, and anyone with former contacts with America was suspect. Many were imprisoned and killed simply because in the past they had known, or had worked for or with, Americans.

The Three-Self Committees fell into the patriotic beat of the times and condemned some former American missionaries, with the hope this might unify the Chinese Christians and also let the government know the Christians were Chinese. To some observers China's Christian leaders were forcing the issue. China's Christians had no idea how much time they had before religion might be banned. It is well known that the communist sees religion as an unnecessary superstition which will one day fade away when the Communist Utopia arrives.

Such forcing of the issue -- denouncing the foreign missionaries, trying to separate China churches and Chinese Christians from foreign associations, and doing away with denominations -- caused many Christians to long even more for the old ways and refuse any suggestion of cooperation with the Three-Self Movement people.

Such was the spirit of Wang Mingdao, an independent pastor in Beijing. He was well loved by his people and had no definite ties to foreign denominations. Wang was pastoring (though he refused the title "pastor") a church that was totally autonomous, taking no funds from overseas, and carrying on its own programs of evangelism and ministry. Wang Mingdao refused to denounce anyone, and when he was brought before the public to be denounced, he uttered not a word. He would not adhere to the new attempts at unity and was thereby falsely judged an enemy of the people and put in prison. He had gone through the same struggle when the Japanese were in Beijing during World War II. Shortly after being jailed Wang was released. He had signed a confession.

He had not been out of prison long when he renounced the confession and was put back in prison. He spent more than 20 years there. After he was released in 1980 he lived out his life in a Shanghai apartment. He died at age 91, July 28, 1991. Christian friends continued to look in on them and help them with marketing and whatever else they may need. He and his wife directed prayer meetings and home Bible studies until their health made it impossible.

Wang Mingdao became the *cause celebre* for all those who for any reason opposed the Three-Self Patriotic Movement. I feel it would grieve Wang's heart if he knew how his unforgiving spirit and attitude had been both used and abused by many to further divide the Christian community of China. It was not Wang Mingdao's intent, but it has been the result. He was a devout fundamentalist and his ministry touched many lives. (For more on Wang Mingdao see *Three of China's Mighty Men* by Leslie Lyall.)

He is not the only person in China to suffer the lost of nearly all things for the cause of Christ. He is just the most well-known. I know the vice-principal of one of the seminaries who spent ten years locked up away from his family and friends. I could give his name, but he asked me not to. Like many others who have not used their sufferings to gain any "fame" or recognition for themselves. They rather thank God for today's miracles and opportunities.

60

During our travels around China from 1982 to 1999 I did not find anyone who would trade the New China for the Old China, nor choose to go back to the former days when a city might have 23 churches sponsored by eight different mission societies or Western denominations. I found this especially true in the city of Hangzhou, but it was also true of most large cities of China.

Pastor and friend Shi Qigui helped me see this reality better than anyone has -- the reality that the new unity in the churches was not something superimposed by some man-made committee but is a direct result of the suffering endured by everyone during the "Cultural Revolution."

During the summer of 1987 I traveled with Shi Qigui and Pastor Lei Tong of the West Shanghai Church on a speaking tour of nine cities and 25 churches in the United States. These men blessed many as they shared their faith and experiences with people from all walks of life. This was the first time since 1949 that a couple of Shanghai preachers have been on such a preaching tour in America. Lei could eat anything, and did! Shi found the fresh salads and Mexican food a bit much for his tastes!

While in a meeting with senior staff members of the Southern Baptist Foreign Mission Board Shi said to them, "If you want to help China, learn where China is in her pilgrimage. China needs friends and co-workers."

Shi Qigui surrendered himself to the Christian ministry while still in middle school in Suzhou. His father before him was a minister. His family was a third-generation Christian family. Following his seminary training he began his ministry with the Muen Church in Shanghai. He served there for 13 years. Then for 13 years he worked in a Shanghai clock factory while the church was closed and the "Cultural Revolution" raged. As he told me this in 1985, I said to him: "You are now in your third 13-year period!" His face lit up with a big smile, and he said, "Yes, 13 years pastoring, then 13 years in a factory, and now I am in my sixth year of my third 13-year cycle. May God give us many more years than just 13 this time."

Shi Qigui is one of the most well-respected men of the city of Shanghai. The 13-year "cycle" is broken. He is now Senior Pastor of the Community Church, known in Chinese as *Guoji Libaitang* on Heng Shan Road. This church was once the American Church and served the American School for foreign children of missionaries, consul and business people.

Shi Qigui, on a more serious note, told how nothing good came from the years of the "Cultural Revolution." "It was a tragic loss of life and energy for China," he said, "but God did some new and wonderful things amid the mess of those years. With church doors closed, pastors and church workers were put into factories and the fields alongside the people." Later, I learned his wife, Fan Peilan, and their son spent most of those years, not at his side, but with other exiles in northern Jiangsu Province.

"Working side by side with our people brought us together in a way we had never known before," Shi related. "No longer were pastors on a high tower looking down on the people's problems and needs; we became one with the people."

He paused and then, looking me straight in the eyes, said: "That is why today our churches are more unified, more one in Spirit than ever before. The Lord broke us and brought us together."

Sharing the heartbeat of men like that has caused me to believe that the churches of China can never go back to the days of Western denominationalism. It would be going backwards. It would be putting in reverse what God has started forward. God has been molding these people for something new, something better, something the whole world needs to experience. Learning the value of mutual respect and cooperation. This more important than any doctrines or church polity that evolved out of the Sixteenth century European Reformation

The churches of China are just that -- churches. There is no Church of China as such. There is no Church of Christ in China, but merely congregations that are thrilled with the opportunities of worship and service after such a long and dark ordeal. A national church, or even a church constitution, has yet to be born. Much work is going into such a project, but other needs command the time of the leaders--needs such as getting the Bible and hymn books published and distributed, training of clergy, and negotiating with officials and individuals to reclaim church properties.

Almost all the churches are of a conservative bent in theology. They carry on their local programs with a great deal of autonomy. They loosely cooperate with one another, helping each other where they can. I have not heard political sermons in church services, but I have heard a concern for human dignity, a free society and the need for the grace and salvation that Jesus Christ offers to all.

In China, Christians are not allowed to instigate preaching services on street corners or evangelize as is the custom of some in Western nations. But, when fellow workers or relatives note the Christian's attitude and life-style, they can tell them why they are different; why they are Christians. This is basic New Testament evangelism. They have no mass evangelistic rallies or famous TV or radio preachers, but they do have a life to share, with those they come in contact with from day to day. That life, lived before others, is still the best form of evangelism known to man.

At the first graduation ceremony in 20 years at the Jinling Union Theological Seminary, June 29, 1985, the graduating seniors chose as their class song, "Living For Jesus A Life That Is True." My colleague, Charles Wilson, said to me after attending this service that "The churches of China will be in good hands with future leaders who live out the message of that song in their ministry."

Wu Gaozi, then vice-chairman of the National China Christian Council, brought the graduation sermon. George Wu (as he is known to Western friends) urged the graduates to offer themselves completely to the Lord, to pray for wisdom to guide them when they are faced with problems, and to learn from Isaiah's preparedness to be sent wherever the Lord wills them to go. George Wu passed away November 26, 1993 at the age of 90.

Principal K.H. Ting urged the graduates to persist in, and continue to be guided by, the principles of the Three-Self

Movement, while on the other hand uniting with all Christians. "Neither should be overemphasized the one at the expense of the other," he said. "The Three-Self Movement was not initiated to frighten or to intimidate people; it is a movement to unite Christians."

The Three-Self Movement is not a church. The organization attempts to help the government authorities understand the advantages of the Christian faith to China's development. Such efforts are hindered if the local Three-Self official himself does not know these things. Ultra-leftist in the church structure can be more damaging than those who run the government. The Christian workers of China have to deal with both.

The post-denominational church of China is also having a difficult time with titles and offices within the church.

The various titles for Christians and church leaders are a carry-over from former years and may need to become more Chinese in use and understanding. The scriptural titles such as *Mushi* (pastor), *Chuandao* (preacher), *Zhanglao* (elder), *Laoshi* (teacher), *Dixiong* (brother), *Zimei* or *Jiemei* (sister), and *Zhujiao* (bishop) are evolving. It is far too early to try to define what these shall come to mean to the peoples of China as the churches develop and grow their own Chinese theology, philosophy of church government, evangelism, and missionary outreach.

The term bishop in China today is more one of respect than authority. I have met four of the first six Protestant bishops in China and they are not superintendents of definite areas. They are spiritual leaders in the New Testament sense.

On June 26, 1988 two Shanghai pastors were dedicated to the office of bishop. They were Sun Yanli of the Muen Church and Shen Yifan of the Community Church. Both have since gone to be with the Lord. Sun Yanli, as has been noted, came out of retirement to persuade Shanghai government officials to return the Muen Church property to the Christians. Shen Yifan died August 12, 1994 as the age of 66. His death was considered even more unfortunate as a preacher in his sixties is not considered old and he was counted on for many years of leadership.

Toward the end of 1988 there were certain foreign Christian groups, mission boards and societies that took renewed interest in carrying the gospel to China. Some of these majored on what they called "target groups." Southern Baptists followed the lead of Assembly of God leaders, Campus Crusades people and Youth With A Mission and other groups to "target" the Minority Nationalities of China.

There are more than 50 of these ethnic peoples in China. The largest being the Hui, or Muslim Nationality. Others of historical note are the Uygers, Koreans, Miao, Tibetans, Manchus and Zhuang. Ignoring the China Christian Council and its work with these peoples, some of the above mentioned foreign mission organizations began in the late 1980s to carry on undercover activities with these "target groups."

Such activity became so arrogant by the International Mission Board of the Southern Baptist Convention that the China Christian Council (CCC) eventually had to request the IMB personnel leave China in 1997. Their "secret" activities included baptizing people in hotel bathrooms, holding meetings and handing out Christian literature on the sly. This kind of activity brings suspicion upon the local Christians and causes the authorities to believe that Christianity as spread by Western nations was not good for China. China of today is not the First century Roman Empire. There is freedom of religion with restrictions in China. Christianity is not banned. Covert missions is not necessary, desirable, nor productive.

Because IMB would not dialogue with the CCC for months, President Han Wenzao wrote requesting they cease their covert activities. He was ignored. Today the best Baptist witness in China is done by the Cooperative Baptist Fellowship (CBF), headed in China by Dr. Ron Winstead and his wife Ina and by individuals who minister at their own expense without Western denominational ties. Ron and Ina teach in the Guangxi University in Nanning, China, and lead summer courses with American volunteers to upgrade the English of the area schools.

Ron spent 17 years as a missionary to Taiwan. He learned the language well and taught Greek and New Testament at the Taiwan Baptist Theological Seminary in Taipei. He joined me while I was China Liaison Director for Southern Baptist's IMB (then known as the Foreign Mission Board). He and Ina taught for years in Shanghai's former Baptist college (*Hujiang Daxue* "Shanghai University") and succeeded me as China Liaison Director before leaving IMB to head up the CBF's China outreach.

For non-Southern Baptists it should be noted that the CBF is not a separate Southern Baptist denomination. It came into being because of the take-over of the SBC by the fundamentalists. It is a fellowship of moderate and caring Baptists who are attempting to stay true to the historical Baptist heritage.

One of the first of Southern Baptist's Journeymen Program that studied Chinese in China was Kim Dickey. (See Chapter Eleven). Miss Dickey spent two years as a language student in Shanghai's Fudan University. She has over ten years of experience working with the churches of China and is now married to John Strong. They live and minister as Presbyterians in Nanjing. Other Baptists who see the importance of ministring as the Chinese see best are Gwen Crotts, Faye Pierson and Lynn Yarbrough.

But others, like the Seventh-Day Adventist denomination, push their own denominational bias; resurrected and directed from abroad as they had before the founding of the People's Republic of China.

Individual Christians have been coming to China for years, unfortunately many of these using the cover of "English teacher" while their primary purpose is to win souls. Some of these even opposing the open and growing churches in their midst. This is not true of the Amity Foundation teacher project nor some other teacher-sending agencies. Be a good teacher and the students will be interested in your God. Be a friend if you expect to win a friend. (For more on this see the Afterword in this book on "So you want to teach or minister in China.")

China university students wonder about foreign Christian teachers who do not even attend the local churches. Other questions I have been asked: "Why do they meet in secret?" "Where do their converts go for spiritual growth once the teacher leaves China?" It is just an appealing adventure for some to work in a covert manner. A study of China history and society has helped many of these to see the error of their ways and begun working openly. Unfortunately such has not been the case with my own Southern Baptists. As the rest of the world enters the 21st century the SBC IMB continue to labor as 19th century foreign missionaries.

Some Chinese leaders of house churches or home meeting points were arrested and even sentenced to prison for preaching against the government, the Party and the China Christian Council. Some were proven to have received funds from Christian groups abroad. Such behavior told the Party and government officials that Christianity still depended upon the west; that Christianity by nature was not just religious but very subversive in nature. Such underground activities do not enhance the work of Christ in China.

The Catholics have more problems than Protestants. This is because of their historical relation with Rome. Many China Catholics desire to be reunited with Rome. Foreign connections of that sort are not permitted in China.

The Union of Catholic Asia News reported Father Shi Wande, Father Su Zhemin and a lay leader Wang Tongshang of the Baoding diocese of Hebei province in north China were arrested in December 1989.

Such developments come not so much from a weak religious policy as from officials in government and Party that have no earthly (or heavenly) idea what religion really is. Many of these officials in the Religious Affairs Bureau and the United Front organization use the rules and laws to control the people rather than help the people. This has been repeatedly voiced by Christian, Buddhist and Muslim religious leaders.

Now as the new century approaches (January 1, 2001) there appear fewer restrictions on the churches of China. They still must work under laws that Americans would never tolerate but this is where God has planted them and this is where they will grow. The gospel can take root in any soil, regardless of how rocky, hard, or parched. Just give it time and not rush it. This is also seen in the attempts to develop a Chinese theology which in the next chapter attempts to explain.

CHAPTER SIX

Prelude To A Chinese Theology

Taking Root Downward: Meeting The Needs of Theological Education

"And they said ... 'Were not our hearts burning within us while He was speaking to us on the road, while He was explaining the Scriptures to us?'"

> --- *The conversation between two believesrs on an Emmaus Road after an encounter with Jesus, as recorded in **Luke 24:32**.*

I can remember many a prayer meeting on the island of Taiwan when Southern Baptist missionaries who had spent many years in China--missionaries like Martha Franks, Bertha Smith, Olive Lawton and Pearl Johnson (1898-1990) -- would pray and ask the Lord of the harvest to send out laborers. They always stressed God's "calling out the called," praying that God would lay it on the hearts of his own people to give themselves to ministry.

This same spirit of prayer continues throughout China as the churches need pastors, church leaders, and helpers as never before. The harvest of believers is great. Many are praying that God will call out, from villages and towns, those already in the churches to take up the challenge of leading tomorrow's churches of China.

When a believer feels he/she has been called of God to a full-time ministry, what do they do? The normal procedure is to seek out the pastor, or a dedicated deacon or elder for direction. Sometimes, it is the other way around. A pastor or church member may notice the warmth and concern of a fellow believer and suggest to them that they pray about the possibility of God's using them in the ministry.

George W. Truett, Southern Baptists' most loved pastor and preacher, came to the ministry this way. Members of his local church in Whitewright, Texas, seeing his possibilities, urged him to leave his teaching profession and enter the ministry. God can use fellow believers in this fashion in China today if they help each other find the gifts of God and use them to his glory.

When the young prospective theological student is clear in his or her mind and heart that their life should be given to a career in Christian ministry there are certain steps that have to be taken. An early step is to take tests. Such tests at the local church level are on church polity and Bible beliefs. An application is made to the nearest seminary or to the national seminary in Nanjing.

Unfortunately, because of a lack of qualified teachers and because they have very limited space, the seminaries can only take a small percentage of those who apply. In 1985, the dean and vice-principal of Jinling Seminary, Chen Zemin, told me: "For the Fall term we have 450 applications from new students who want to study here, but we can accept only 50 of these." Professor Chen looked down as he continued. "Pray with us that we accept the students God has chosen. We cannot afford any mistakes in choosing those who should be here and those who should not be here."

It is such concern that has led to the opening of regional seminaries and Bible training centers. These schools offer some help in preparing students for both today's and tomorrow's church. Some of the seminaries have grown from short-term lay training institutes and night schools, while others have begun as full-time theological training centers. China has a shortage of college graduates, so most of these students have only finished middle school. The seminaries are not yet degree-granting institutions. That will come as they develop and grow to that point. The seminaries will be related in some way to the National Council on Education, and when degrees are granted they will be recognized and respected as equal to other institutional degrees.

The Jinling Union Theological Seminary resumed operations on March 1, 1981, in Nanjing. Bishop K. H. Ting, was named principal. Classes began that first year with 47 students and about a dozen faculty members. On June 29, 1985, the first graduation in 20 years was a festive occasion. A total of 95 students graduated from the two, three, or four-year courses.

Some of these students, upon finishing their course of study, returned to their home churches, while others remained to do further study. Two of the 1985 graduates went to help teach in the newly opened Zhongnan (South Central) Seminary in Wuhan. One graduate went to the Fujian Seminary to do the same. A married couple who completed their study in Nanjing went to the seminary in Guangzhou.

The course of study at Jinling is divided into four basic areas: Biblical, Pastoral, Historical, and Theological. During the first year, all students are expected to read the Bible in its entirety. Music and art are stressed, and the seminary choir is well known in East China for its spirit and ability. Courses in civics, socialism, Chinese language, history and culture also are taught by guest lecturers and professors from nearby Nanjing University.

Three mornings a week the Jinling students and faculty gather for morning prayers in the chapel. Sometimes a student leads the devotions. More often a teacher or visiting pastor will speak. One morning when I was visiting the chapel, a Jiangsu pastor spoke on the tremendous challenge China holds for these future leaders.

In the midst of the message, Pastor Wu became very personal with us. Recalling days long gone, he said, "I remember years ago hearing the evangelist John Sung [Song Shangjie, an outstanding evangelist in China and Asia until his death in 1944]. John Sung was preaching in a series of meetings in Tianjin. Sung told us that if all our religion was just between our ears, just in our heads, we would best stop preaching and find other work."

The elder statesman-pastor paused and looked over the crowded chapel. It appeared to me that all 284 students and most faculty members were present. Pastor Wu continued his recollection of the evangelist's message: "China needs you, 'but not with head religion only,' Sung told the congregation. You must lead with your heart. You must prepare your heart and your head to meet the tremendous challenge our churches offer."

Later the same day, I was asked if I would speak in the chapel service the following Monday. I really could not believe my ears. I was there to learn from them. What could I possibly say of any value. I accepted anyway at once and spent the weekend wondering whether I had been right in accepting. Such a challenge and responsibility began to overwhelm me. I have always considered any speaking engagement important. Each demands that what is said fit that particular place and people. I have never been one for using retread sermons.

That weekend I wondered what I, a foreigner, who knows so little of the Chinese seminary student's situation and needs, could possibly say in that chapel service. And would they understand my fractured Texas style of Shandong mandarin?

It has been my conviction that the foreigner should spend most of his time in China listening, not talking. Just to sit at the feet of some of China's spiritual giants, to learn from them, was more important to me than speaking. But there comes a time, when we are requested to share, that we must speak. Later I was reminded of what David Paton wrote: "Nothing is more important than to know what appointment God has made for us; and no appointment is more worth keeping."

So I spent the weekend reading again from the gospel of John, especially chapter sixteen. In this chapter, Jesus is over and over assuring his friends of his presence and concern for them, offering encouragement for them as they approach the fact of his leaving them. In the Chinese Bible, Jesus tells his disciples that before too much time has passed they will not see him; but then after an interval they will see him again. In this personal way, Jesus was saying what all his friends needed to hear. All they needed to know was wrapped up in those simple sentences. He was going away, meaning the cross; he was coming again, meaning his resurrection would follow his death. To Jesus, his death and his resurrection were always one event. The apparent defeat of death was to be followed by the rousing resurrection to new life. The darkness of the valley but heralds the brightness of the mountain peaks. God had given me a message of encouragement.

What may have been just another morning chapel service to many of those who listened that Monday morning was, to me, the experience of a lifetime. In nearly 30 years of preaching the wonderful story of our Lord in the Chinese language, I had never experienced such encouragement of the Holy Spirit in what He said through me and the way He did it. I was the one who went away encouraged.

A month or so later, while visiting the Jinling campus again, one young lady, a student, greeted me with a big smile.

"You spoke so well last month," she said, in perfect English.

As I gave the common Chinese expressions of polite refusal of such a gracious remark, for what I had said was far short of what it should have been, my heart was overcome that anyone would remember I was even there, much less spoke, and spoke well! The young lady, Gao Ying, was the first from the seminary to study abroad and is now a most active ordained minister in Beijing.

Then, as Gao Ying went on across the campus, she added in Chinese, "You must have studied the Bible somewhere, for what you said of our Lord is true. We have found it so."

Other contact, formal and informal, with students in ten of China's seventeen seminaries, encourages me that they are God's choice people and that he is preparing them for the challenge of a lifetime -- a life of witness and ministry in the fastest growing church on earth today.

When New Testament professor Zhao Zhien asked me to speak in chapel that day, it gave me a chance to get to know him a little better. I learned over tea that he was a widower, with a grown son and daughter living in Nanjing. He was in his mid-fifties and has served both as former pastor at the Mo Chou Road church in Nanjing and seminary teacher since graduation from the Nanjing Theological Seminary (a forerunner of Jinling Seminary).

Zhao loves to preach, and he speaks regularly in the open churches and in the house churches or meeting points. His experience was refreshing to me as he told of the way both the open churches and the house churches worked together in and around Nanjing. There were too few churches re-opened which caused many of the people to continue worshipping in homes. On July 28, 1985, while we were visiting the area Mr. Xu was being ordained to pastor the Da Chang Church north of the Changjiang (Yangzi River). Mr. Xu, now Pastor Xu, is a retired engineer and had been the shepherd for the Da Chang Meeting Point for some years. In October of 1985, the congregation began building their first church-like structure, a worship center that better meets their needs.

A lot of Zhao's time in 1985 was spent visiting remote areas and finding ways the seminaries can be cooperative -- seeking ways that Jinling can help the regional seminaries.

"Then you have traveled a good bit?" I asked him.

It was then he shared what to him was one of his most memorable trips. "It was in November of 1982," Zhao began "when a seminary classmate of mine, Shen Cheng'en (Editor of *Tian Feng*, the national Protestant paper, and a pastor of the Community Church in Shanghai), went to the mountains of Yunnan province to help ordain some new pastors."

He poured some more tea for both of us and wondered if I really cared to hear about the trip. I assured him I did.

He continued: "In Yunnan, near the Vietnam border, there were 12 candidates for the ministry. They came from nine counties to be ordained. Ten of them were from the mountain tribes of the Miao, Yi, Lisu and Jingpo (Ching Po) nationalities."

As Zhao shared this, I reflected on the *shaoshu minzu*, China's Minority Nationalities. These people only make up 6.5 percent of China's population. Some 55 people groups from Koreans, Manchus and Mongolians in the north to the Uygers and Tibetans of the west to the Lisu, Miao and Zhuang of the southwest that Zhao was talking about. These are some of the people that the SBC IMB was so intent upon "targeting" in their covert Western evangelism. At that time I was unaware such was about to take place. But here I was hearing what the CCC actually was doing among a people the IMB claimed was ignored by the CCC.

Since most of China's border areas are populated with these nationalities, it is good business for the government to keep them happy. They are a good buffer. And this is another reason NOT to have clandestine work among them. Revolts so easily begin in these border areas. For the past ten years there have been bloody riots in the far western area of Xinjiang, a strong Muslim or Hui area.

In Kunming, the capital of Yunnan Province, there is a special university for these various nationalities called the Institute of the Nationalities. Almost every province has such a school but this one is special since it is in the heart of so many minorities. Baylor University began early in the 1980s an exchange program of students and teachers with this institution and with the Second Foreign Language Institute in Beijing.

With another round of tea, Zhao continued, "The 12 men to be ordained had been recommended by their own church communities after considerable prayer. This was followed by an examination by the Yunnan Provincial Christian Council." One thing he added really came home to me: "The candidates had to be familiar with the Bible and have a good reputation both inside and outside the church community."

Professor Zhao echoed the plea of many, that "the harvest is great, but the workers are too few!" He went on to tell how tears came to the eyes of the old and young alike as they parted. "Old men stretched out their calloused hands and, while holding us firmly, thanked us for coming. I could only thank God for such grace to allow me to witness the faith of these people in Yunnan."

Later on a 1987 trip to Kunming, Yunnan province, Pastor Gu Huaikong told of plans for a seminary for the nationalities of Yunnan and Guangxi. The school became a reality in 1989.

As a Baptist I was naturally interested to learn that Chen Zemin, dean of the Jinling Seminary, was of the Baptist tradition and a graduate of the old Shanghai University (Hujiang Daxue), a school founded in 1905 as a joint effort between the Northern

Baptist Convention (now the American Baptist Church) and the Southern Baptist Convention.

Chen, speaking impeccable English, introduced me to two of the seminary professors, Wang Weifan and Mo Ruxi, as we settled down to cups of hot tea and theological sharing that was a bit beyond me; but it was good to get a taste of what the seminary is trying to do in training tomorrow's leaders. "We have on our faculty a good mixture of opinions," Chen said. "We are not trying to teach one kind of theology, such as liberal or conservative. We have teachers of both persuasions, and we let the students hear everything and decide for themselves what is most useful in their ministry."

To some this might sound like a cop-out, as though they were not willing to make a stand. China Protestant's approach is more realistic and scriptural than the divisions brought on by the arguments and politics between the so-called liberals, moderates and conservative elements of many American denominations today.

The church leaders in China do not agree on a lot of matters, but those who love the church above all else are working at mutual respect in a Christ-like manner.

The seminary teachers share from their heart what God has given them. The students receive what the Holy Spirit can use in their life and ministry. Mutual respect will go a long way in bringing Christians of various traditions closer together. This could be one of the future blessings the churches of China will help the world to experience.

In Montreal, Canada, in 1981, Professor Chen shared something of what was important to the emerging churches of China. He said:

> Chinese Christians, while working shoulder to shoulder with our compatriots in this common task are sincerely trying to relate the Christian faith and commitment to the great experience the Chinese people are going through. Our church is as yet small and young, and we have many problems and difficulties, but we can say now that there is a Chinese church, a

`church' coming of age, not quite in the ecclesiological sense, but a viable community committed to the Christian faith. During the three decades of struggle and experimentation, we have gained some theological insights that we would like to share with our fellow Christians abroad.

Our point of departure is to opt for the people, to opt for the welfare of our country, and to opt for a social system that is more just and humane than anything the Chinese people have seen in their history of over four thousand years.

The People's Republic is by no means perfect. There is much to improve. There are defects and mistakes and, consequently, tragedies.

Professor Chen distanced himself from the Latin American Liberation Theology when he said, at the same meeting in Montreal,

Our theological task is not liberation as such, in the Latin American sense, but reconciliation -- to be reconciled to and identified with the Chinese people as a whole, from whom we had been alienated, for the carrying on of our task of liberation for the further betterment of our society; and at the same time, to be reconciled to God, from whom the human race has been alienated and with whom we all yearn to be united through the mediating mystery of the incarnate Christ in the endless course of human history.

Professor Mo Ruxi was an English professor and Associate Dean of Studies at Jinling Seminary. She is a diminutive giant, if such an adjective can be used. She, like most Christians in China, urge facing the future rather than dealing constantly with the past.

Wang Weifan, a teacher, pastor and friend, is also a poet, and one of his poems was put to music by Shanghai's Jingling Church pastor Lin Shengben. It is one of the many beloved hymns in the new China hymnal, *Hymns of Praise*. The first phrase in the hymn "Winter Is Past" (*Dongtian yi wang*), was used as the name of the Southern Baptist Foreign Mission Board (now IMB) film on Christianity in China that was filmed in East China during the fall of 1985. The hymn was inspired by a Bible passage (Song of Solomon 2:10-14) and relates the joy of God's love and life following a great tribulation. Wang Weifan wrote these verses in 1957 (English translation by Ewing W. Carroll, Jr.):

> The winter has passed, the rain is o'er
> Earth is a-bloom, songs fill the air.
> Linger no more, why must you wait;
> Rise up my love, come follow me.
>
> O Lord thy face I long to see,
> Thy still small voice, reveal to me.
> Thy tender care, thy joy so dear
> O precious dove with me be near.
>
> O my belov'd, I'll follow thee
> Far from the rocks, the hills and sea.
> Midst all the song and blossoms new
> In your firm steps, I'll follow you.

The chorus Wang wrote 25 years later:

> Jesus my Lord, my love, my all,
> Body and soul, forever yours.
> In dale so dark, I long for thee.
> Spring has returned, Abide with me.

Wang Weifan's prose is as beautiful as his poetry. He wrote the following based on Hebrews 12:1 for All Saints Day (Trans. by Janice and Philip Wickeri from Wang's book, Lillies of the Field, Revised Edition, 1989, p. 64):

78

Why should we fear hiding in catacombs or roaming the far corners of the earth? Why fear the lion's jaws or the knife's blade?

This road we walk is strewn with flowers stained red by blood shed in the cause of justice. Our companions on this road include both heroes and criminals, saints as well as sinners.

We need not lament having paid out too much of ourselves in life, nor should we regret that at the moment of death, we are left with nothing. Every drop of blood, each bead of sweat, is a seed buried deep within the earth. Though we cannot harvest the fruits of our labors ourselves, others will come to take up the task, and they, too, will have successors.

Rose-colored in the morning light, glowing softly at dusk, clouds of witness drift across the deep blue skies. They yearn for that constant, enduring city, but they never lose affection for the native land they have left behind.

The tremendous need for pastors and church workers has been the main concern of the China Christian Council. Lay-training institutes spring up across the land, trying to meet immediate needs with short-term Bible and church leadership courses. Some of these have advanced so rapidly and well that they have grown into regional theological seminaries or Bible colleges.

The first of these regional seminaries to open was in Shenyang, Liaoning province, October 20, 1982. The Shenyang Seminary was renamed Dongbei (Northeast) Seminary in 1987. The first year the seminary had 54 students, including seven Koreans. Liaoning borders Korea, and there are many Koreans living in the area.

With very little space and hardly a book to call their own, the pastors of the area led in the opening of the Dongbei Theological Seminary with the faith that God would provide. The school has now grown to include students from the three northeastern provinces of Jilin, Heilongjiang and Liaoning.

Pastor Zhang Shangmin served as the first principal and Ms. Lu Zhibin is now principal. She became the second woman to lead a China seminary.

The following spring, church leaders in Beijing launched the Beijing Theological Seminary with seven students. Christians and churches are fewer in Beijing than in other cities of its size. Some give the figure of 6,000 Christians there. Three churches have been reopened for worship and religious activities in the nation's capital. For some years negotiations have been going on to have the Yanjing University School of Religion buildings and campus returned to the China Christians for use as a seminary.

Another seminary opened in nearby Tianjin, a former treaty port, two hours by train southeast of Beijing. Pastor Liu Qingfen led the Tianjin Seminary that met in the church on Binjiang Road in the Heping District. This school united with the Beijing Seminary to become the Yanjing Theological Seminary in Beijing. The Yanjing Seminary began classes in September 1986 in a renovated London Missionary Society church on Dongdan Dajie. During the 1990s the seminary moved to a new campus.

In September 1983 two more local China Christian Councils ventured out on faith to open similar schools in their areas--one in Southwest China and one in Southeast China. The Fujian Theological Seminary opened its doors to 40 students on September 13, 1983. Classes are held in the Hua Xiang (Flower Lane) Church in Fujian's capital city of Fuzhou. In September of 1986 the seminary began holding classes for their 81 students in the YMCA while a new campus was being constructed. The only book they had in their meager library was a Bible. What better place to begin a library!

The library has grown with Chinese and English books donated by friends and co-workers in the area. Bishop Moses Hsieh (Xue Pingxi) is principal and presided over the school's first graduation of more than 60 students in June of 1985. One of that year's graduates went on to do advanced study at the Jinling Seminary in Nanjing. One graduate went to the Huadong Seminary in Shanghai for more advanced study. Others returned to their churches in and around Fujian province to share in the ministry of the churches that sent and sponsored them.

On September 19, 1983, one week after the Fujian school opened, the Chengdu Lay Training Institute was upgraded to a regional seminary and renamed the Sichuan Theological Seminary. Students attend from three provinces, Sichuan, Guizhou and Yunnan.

Jody, my wife, was in Chengdu at the close of the Sichuan Seminary's first year of study. She was most impressed with the faculty and student body. She likes everything about Sichuan. In addition to the gracious people of Sichuan I think it may be the hot peppers and highly seasoned food that make her want to keep going back.

In September 1985 three new seminaries opened their doors to students in the cities of Shanghai, Hangzhou and Wuhan. The Huadong (East China) Seminary opened September 11 in Shanghai using the educational building of the Grace Church. I sat in the balcony for most of the four-hour opening ceremony, video taping the ceremony. Qi Qingcai, senior pastor at Grace and the chairman of the new seminary board, brought a challenging message to the 40 students. Bishop Sun Yanli was the first president or principal.

In just one year the Huadong Seminary had outgrown the Grace Church property and in July of 1986 moved to new and larger quarters in the center of Shanghai at the Muen Church. The student body grew to 80. In 1989 the seminary moved a third time into two new buildings built for the seminary at number 71 Wu Yuan Road, south of the Hilton Hotel and north of the Community Church. (Go on the Internet and see the new campus layout at www.laotao.org/mission)

In all the regional seminaries and Bible colleges local pastors teach the religious courses while area university professors help with courses in Chinese culture, language history. Since June 4, 1989 seminary students, like all university students, must spend time in class "studying" the most recent speech by Communist Party General Secretary Jiang Zemin. Most students I talked to viewed such sessions as a waste of time.

81

South of Shanghai, three and a half hours by fast train, the Zhejiang Theological Seminary opened in the ancient city of Hangzhou. Zhejiang Province has the largest number of Christians of any area in China. There are now more than one million believers in more than a 1000 churches and home Meeting Points. This total represents more Christians than were in all of China in 1949. Classes are held in the lower floor activities rooms of the Si Cheng Church. This former Presbyterian church is now named in memory and honor of its first Chinese pastor. Francis Fan (Fan Aishi) is principal. He is a 1940 graduate of the Nanjing Theological Seminary and has pastored in Shanghai, Ningbo and Hangzhou.

When the pastors of Zhejiang sent out word to the churches they were planning to open a seminary the response in offerings exceeded by three times the proposed goals. The people of the churches of this coastal province made it clear with their prayers and gifts they want to train church leaders for the future.

West of Shanghai, an hour or so by plane, the Zhongnan (South Central) Seminary opened in the tri-cities area of Wuhan on the Changjiang (Yangtze River). This was in May, 1985. Principal Liu Nianfen, the first woman seminary principal, came back to China from study abroad in 1951. When plans were in the making for this seminary, Ms. Liu went to work on the Wuhan University faculty and staff to find teachers for the non-religious courses. She was successful, and the students are getting top-notch professors in world history and Chinese history, culture and language. The seminary also offers some English classes. When the school opened--with 41 students -- Principal Liu was ably assisted by two fine graduates of the Jinling Seminary who assist on the faculty along with local pastors.

In the fall of 1986 two additional area seminaries opened. One in Hefei, capital of Anhui province and one in the southern city of Guangzhou (Canton). Then vice principal and now principal Harold Huang (Huang Guangyao) invited me to the opening ceremony September 25, 1986 but my schedule made it impossible to attend. Since Hong Kong is only 90 miles from Guangzhou a number of people from various churches and denominations attended the opening held in the former Dongshan Baptist Church.

On October 10, 1987 the Shandong Theological Seminary was opened in Jinan with Bishop Stephen Wang (Wang Shenyin) as the first principal. Out of short-term Bible courses has grown yet another school, this one called Shengjing Xueyuan (Bible College) of Shaanxi in Xi'an. Mr. Tian Jingfu was principal and the school met in the Shan Yuan Christian Church. Mention has already been made of the Yunnan Seminary in Kunming for the Nationalities that opened in 1989. Pastor Zhang Xianzhou is principal. Eleven ethnic groups make up the 56-student body now studying in Kunming. More seminaries opened during the 1990s bringing the total to seventeen.

Leaders of theological education in China met in August of 1985 to try and coordinate training of seminary and Bible school students. Curriculum needs were uppermost on everyone's minds. It was decided that one of the most urgent needs for training a new generation of church leaders would be the writing and publishing of suitable textbooks. Books that grew from China's history, society and mission.

The first four seminary textbooks came off the press in June, 1988. They were: *First and Second Corinthians*, by Wang Weifan; *Meditations on the Song of Songs*, by Wang Zhen; *Pastoral Ministry*, by Peng Shengyong; and *Church History*, by Zhao Zhikang. The overall editorial direction is by a committee of three: Bishop Shen Yifan of Shanghai, Chen Zemin, Nanjing Seminary vice-principal, and teacher-pastor Wang Weifan.

Five more textbooks are due out in 1990: *Introduction to the New Testament* by Luo Zhenfang; *Bible Geography* by Chen Shiyi; *Studies in Acts* by Zhao Zhien; *A History of Israel* by Yu Dingying; and *The Pentateuch* by Wang Weifan.

These books have come from years of study and teaching of the subjects. Most of the seminary teachers would be retired years ago by western standards. They seem to have been granted extra years and strength to better prepare the next generation of church workers, whether clergy or laity.

83

The strain on these seminary professors, whose average age would be between 65 and 70, would be unheard of outside of China. Most of them help in churches on weekends, and some are full-time pastors who help with seminary teaching during the week. All have more than they can possibly do. I find in talking with them that they are not thinking of retirement, nor are they thinking of an easy way to spend their last years. This of course is a constant temptation, put on them sometimes by well-meaning and loving family members, to slow down and rest a bit. They would like that. It is only human. They are, in a most unassuming manner, glad to have a part in this new day in China. They are excited to share, to visit, to teach and preach, for they know what it is to be forbidden to do these things. These men, like the prophet Amos of Old Testament days, know injustice when they see it. They have lived it and they have an experience that must be transplanted into the minds and hearts of this new generation of preacher-students if there is to be hope for tomorrow.

For some years selected students have been sent abroad by the China Christian Council for advanced study so they can help these provincial, regional and area seminaries and Bible colleges.

In the fall of 1989 Jody and I were asked to help with a group of seven students slated to study abroad in 1990. Several English teachers helped them with conversation, composition, worship and culture. Our contribution was the introduction of English theological terms and concepts.

The seven students graduated from four China seminaries. After their overseas study, plans were for them to take up some of the teaching responsibilities in various seminaries. Wang Xiaoyin, Sun Jiaji and Ms. Zhang Yuezhu are graduates of the Dongbei Seminary in Shenyang; He Beien and Ms. Chen Yuqing are graduates of the Huadong Seminary in Shanghai; Wu Jiade is a graduate of Yanjing Seminary in Beijing; and Ms. He Huibing is a graduate of the Jinling Seminary of Nanjing. Ms. He Huibing taught Christian Art at Jinling Seminary and contributed several sketches for the third edition of this book. She now lives in America.

84

Christian art has had a greater emphasis at Nanjing because of the tireless efforts of artist Dr. He Qi. Creator of the biblical paper cuts and works of art unequaled anywhere.

At any one time somewhere in China a short-term Bible and church training course is in progress. These are sponsored by local Christian Councils and generally led by local pastors. Jinling Seminary has not only shared their faculty with the provinces but sent evangelistic teams into the rural areas during vacations or weekends.

From 1979 through 1984 an average of one church a day was being reopened or newly built. Since 1987 the China Christian Council has made rural church development a major concern and emphasis. Newly built churches are colorful and different from place to place. Every month the *Tian Feng* magazine has colorful pictures of new churches. Some of these can be seen on the Tao Mission Forum web site: <www.laotao.org/mission>

A correspondence course, called *Han Shou*, with 1000 enrolled began in September 1989, with Pastor Kong Xiangjin and four assistants carrying the program. Rev. Kong also serves as pastor in a northern Jiangsu province city.

Every year rural church workers are brought to Nanjing for a year of study. Evangelist-pastor-professor Ms. Jiang Peifen gives the majority of her time to this lay leaders training course, called *Pei Xun Ban*. The courses have been successful for a number of years. During the 1989-90 school year there were 62 laymen and women studying at the Jinling Seminary. They take off from their work and support themselves or are supported by the church that sends them. When they return to their village and township ministries they can give more effective service to their people and community.

The Jinling Seminary is the only seminary presently working on a graduate level with a full-time staff. In addition to Principal K. H. Ting and Dean Chen Zemin, Zhao Zhi'en, Jiang Peifen, Wang Weifan and Mo Ruxi already mentioned are capable men like Luo Zhenfang in New Testament and Greek; Sun Hanshu and Xu Rulei in church history; and Xu Dingxing in Old Testament and Hebrew.

Jinling Seminary has a leading part in the Institute of Religious Studies of Nanjing University. When seminary professors have given lectures on aspects of Christianity at this Institute hundreds of university students have attended the classes. Such courses are rare in China and an eye-opener for the students.

In addition to the *Jinling Shenxue Hz (Nanjing Theological Review),* edited by Bao Shimming, there is a novel and interesting trend taking shape in theological study and writing practically unknown to the non-Chinese-speaking world. Liu Xiaofeng, of Tianjin and Shenzhen, found God and a love of theology from reading Russian novels and books. He has had published in Chinese literary journals ten articles on Christian theologians. Some of them early Russian theologians not well-known to the English-speaking world.

Professor Liu has written a book *Salvation and Free Spirit ("Zhengjiu Yu Xiao Yao")* that received critical acclaim in the national literary journal *Dushu.* Professor Liu was a man who found God apart from anybody's establishment of religion or church, Chinese or foreign.

Others like Liu, often called "Cultural Christians," some unbaptized, some with little knowledge of current or historical church trends are going to the Bible and making some startling and exciting waves for the long neglected intellectual believer in China. Some of the best theological writing in China today is coming from men like Liu Xiaofeng.

A few of the books I have scanned myself are: *Hebrew Culture; Problems of Religion in Chinese Socialist Stage; History of Religious Thinking in China; Bible Study; Christian Philosophy; and New Thoughts About the Bible.* The English titles of these books are my own and not necessarily the English titles the various authors would put on them. They are all published in China and are grabbed up eagerly by a spiritually and intellectually hungry readership.

As theology evolves in China the words of K. H. Ting in his book *How To Study the Bible*, written in 1980, take on even more importance. He wrote:

In our Church today, there are still people who unfortunately don't have a high opinion of theology. They view theology either as something harmful to faith or as a branch of secular learning which is not helpful for faith. We must reclaim theology's reputation.

If we think of the Bible as a beautiful painting, then theology is a clearly drawn map. Both of these are important.

What is theology? Theology is the summary and systemization of the spiritual insights which successive generations of Christians from many different cultural backgrounds have received from God. Its function is to guide us in our spiritual quest. If theology does not arise out of the experience of the Church, then it becomes inflexible dogma. But if experience neglects the guidance of theology, then it remains primitive and easily prone to subjectivist abuses. The purpose of theology is to direct our seeking along the right path so that we may not be led astray.

It is the responsibility of theology to examine and protect the precious resources accumulated by the whole Church in past generations, and to guide the lives of individual churches and Christians. ... Without the guidance of Church doctrines, how could we come to full and precise understanding of the whole Bible, avoiding all kinds of biases and heresies? Depending only upon our aimless wandering through the vast world of the Bible, how would we be able to bypass the pitfalls and arrive at the truth?

CHAPTER SEVEN

Tea and Tears
Bearing Fruit Upward:
Meeting Spiritual Needs

The Christians "were constantly devoting themselves to the apostles' teaching and to fellowship, to the breaking of bread and to prayer. And day by day continuing with one mind in the temple, praising God and having favor with all the people. And the Lord was adding to their number day by day those who were being saved."

--- Acts 2:42, 46, 47.

The little old grandmother stuck her head inside her pastor's office door and, after one quick sentence, she was gone. She said, "Nobody loves me; I'm going down to the river, jump in, and die!"

Such a sudden message jolted Pastor Shi Qigui from his desk, and he was up and after her. Catching her at the Hankou Street gate of the Muen Church, he convinced her to come back in and sit down and to talk to him a bit more about her suicide plan. He hoped to persuade her to give up her ideas of jumping into the Huangpu River.

Pastor Shi poured her a cup of tea and tried to let her know she was loved. Shanghai is not an easy place to live. Particularly for the elderly, it is getting increasingly difficult to manage in a city that is one of the world's largest--a city that is not prepared for such growth. For more than 30 years very few apartment buildings were added to the city.

After some tea and tears, she shared what was breaking her heart--what had made her give up on living. She had tried all these years to be a good Christian, she said, but now she just did not seem to be able to do anything right anymore.

"You see," she related, as she got to the point finally, "I have this grandson; he's a good boy, but his wife is too much! We live in the same small room with just a curtain between the two sides of the room."

Taking a sip of tea, she looked at the pastor and continued: "This granddaughter-in-law of mine hit me today. I can't go back there; it is not a home for me. She has been threatening to run me off. No matter how I tried, and oh, how I tried, I could not please her."

"You pray for her?" Pastor Shi asked.

"Yes, I do. I pray for her every day. Loud too!"

It was easy for the pastor to imagine the dear old lady kneeling by her bed and lifting her voice loud in prayer, naming off, one by one, the granddaughter's sins and shortcomings.

The young girl was not a Christian and had little understanding of what her husband's grandmother was doing. She had finally had enough. She struck her. Grandmother just could not face such humiliation any longer. She had headed for the Huangpu.

Pastor Shi could see the problem. He and Fan Peilan, his wife, when the Muen Church opened in 1979 lived in a one-room apartment almost like the attic of the church (Today they have a nice apartment far from their church, which helps in getting needed rest). They had little privacy. He felt fortunate that he and his wife did not have to share their one room with anyone else. But many people did. There were some people in Shanghai who had only a cot or shelf on which to sleep, and then for only eight or ten hours. It was rented out to someone else for the next eight or ten hours. But it was a place to sleep--more than lots of people had in this crowded city.

"Might you pray a bit softer?" Pastor Shi asked, softly himself, to help her think it over a bit. "There is just that thin curtain between your loud praying voice and that poor girl on the other side who is not understanding a word and who is thinking it is abuse. God is not hard of hearing, you know."

Tactfully, he got her to agree to put off the river jump until later--and to go home and see if a soft word and softer prayers might not turn things around.

The little old grandmother determined to give her pastor's suggestions a try. She would go back to her half-room home and use some tact and quieter prayers. She was not sure it would work, but Pastor Shi was persuasive. He has a convincing way with little old grandmothers.

As she made her way out the gate and out toward Xizang Zhong Road, Pastor Shi smiled as he waved good-bye. He urged her to be sure and come first to the church any time she might be on her way to the river to jump in and die.

About six months later, the little old woman was all smiles as she came out of the Sunday worship service at Muen Church. She took Shi Qigui's hand in her excitement and rattled off in the Shanghai dialect the wonderful news: "Not only is there peace in our flat, but the wife of my grandson has promised to come with me to church next Sunday. She wants to see what made me so quiet and different! Thank you, pastor. Praise God."

Such is one story in the life of a Shanghai pastor. There are many more like this one. The more than 129 churches in Shanghai, plus hundreds of Meeting Points of all sizes, presents a tremendous challenge to the pastors and people of these communities. Meeting these spiritual needs is much like it is anywhere. Human nature being what it is, a pastor must be as wise as a serpent and as harmless as a dove. He must be a good listener and enter into the daily life of his community. He must know what his people face day after day. He must know the pressures they are under--the fears and doubts that come in the night. Ivory towers are off limits to pastors in China.

In 1986 Shanghai pastor John M. K. Jiang (Jiang Menguang) told me an interesting experience he had. He said: "Recently I was visited in my church office by the heads of two different Residential Area Committees." Such committees are the most democratic, grass roots organizations in the People's Republic of China. They are usually headed by communist cadres.

"Both visiting cadres wanted me to help them do some ideological work among the masses. Such a request never entered my mind. I never dreamed that communist cadres would come to a Christian pastor with such a request," Pastor Jiang said.

The first cadre to visit Jiang told him of an on-going quarrel between a mother and her daughter-in-law. The neighbors had tried to help them resolve their differences but had managed only to make matters worse. The neighbors had called in the cadres to see if they could help.

"It was then," Jiang said, "that the cadres noticed a Bible on the table in the home and asked if the mother was a Christian. She told them she was. That was when the cadre decided to seek me out to see if I could help them calm the family--and help the neighborhood regain a little peace and quiet. I was glad to do that kind of ideological work among the masses!"

Pastor John Jiang had 25 years of teaching experience behind him before he was able to get back into the ministry, his first love. He said he often wondered what good he was doing teaching middle school students while his training and heart was in the ministry. It was not long after he left teaching and became a pastor at Huxi Church that he got his answer. One morning after a service, several of his former students--who were now studying in universities--stopped him and said, "Now we know the secret." Jiang had no idea what they were talking about. Secret? What secret? Then they told him that, when he was their middle school teacher, they often wondered among themselves why he was so kind to them -- why he went out of his way to help them. Now, after hearing him preach in the church service, they said, "We know your secret. There is something in the Christian faith that makes a person kind, even more useful to his world."

Those 25 years of school teaching were not wasted! The sermons Jiang preached with his life of kindness and helpfulness to others spoke more forcefully than all his pulpit sermons might ever speak. He had the background to be an able pastor. He could even do "ideological work" among the masses of the community. He went on to tell me of the second cadre who came seeking his help. It was a similar experience to the first.

"The second Residential Area Committee head's problem involved a Christian widow suffering from the last painful stages of cancer." I could tell, as Jiang talked, that he knew something of the suffering she was going through. He went on to say: "The cadre told me that this retired worker refused to go to the hospital or accept any help. It was then he said he found out she was a Christian. The cadre hoped I would help persuade her to go to the hospital for some treatment or at least for something to ease her pain."

Jiang said he could still remember the cadre's words. "Pastor," the cadre had said, "We Communists don't know if there is any contradiction between your religious beliefs and medicine, but help us persuade the widow to go to the hospital. She is so pitiful and in so much pain."

"In both these experiences," Pastor Jiang told me, "God opened my spiritual eyes to see that there are many more good opportunities for spreading the good news of Jesus Christ than I ever thought possible."

Pastor Lin Shengben of the Jingling Church of Shanghai divides his time between his church in Shanghai and the new Zhejiang Theological Seminary in Hangzhou. He gives almost equal time to both ministries. When Lin learned I was a Baptist, he asked me if I knew one Eugene Hill. I said, yes, for Hill was a retired Southern Baptist missionary who years ago taught in the Graves Theological Seminary in Guangzhou. That was where Lin knew him. "He was one of my teachers a long time ago," Pastor Lin said.

Lin and his wife are talented musically. He has written the music to a number of hymns now used in China. He wrote the music to Wang Weifan's hymn "Winter Is Past." Mrs. Lin has written the words to much of Pastor Lin's music.

Pastor Lin Shengben is one of four editors who have helped to formulate the *Hymns of Praise*, the first hymnal since 1949 to be made available throughout China. In May of 1983, 200,000 copies were published jointly by the Three-Self Committee and the CCC. The hymnal already has gone through many additional printings. A musical note edition of the hymnal came out December 1985. That edition gave author's names and dates and is a useful addition to the growing music appreciation in the churches.

Spiritual needs are met so much better with music. Another hymn writer I met in Nanjing is Cephas Hsu (Xu Jifa) who now lives in the USA. In a beautiful hymn of praise, Xu Jifa relates the joy of being set free of bonds and of being allowed to return to his family, home and church. In everything he saw the wonderful hand of God. My translation lacks the beauty of the Chinese original: "To Our Lord We Rejoice And Sing"

To our Lord we rejoice and sing
Bountiful fields, flowers a-glow
The fishes fly, the birds soar high,
Blue-green oceans, brilliant sun-rays.
To our Lord we rejoice and sing
In every mountain, fresh flowing streams
The Lord gives life, prosperous life
All is glorious, all is beautiful.

To our Lord we rejoice and sing.
In all the seasons,
The singing never ceases.
His grace and love, marvelously
Encouraging all people's hearts.

Chorus:
Praise to our Father!
Thanksgiving to Him!
He gives greatest happiness to us
My happy heart does sing without ceasing
To our Lord we rejoice and sing.
To our Lord we rejoice and sing.

Joining Pastor Lin as editors of *Hymns of Praise* were Pastor Shi Qigui, mentioned earlier; Cao Shengjie, Associate General Secretary of the China Christian Council and member of Grace Church of Shanghai; and Hong Luming, organist and widow of Bishop Shen Yifan of the Community Church of Shanghai.

My knowing these four people personally makes the *Hymns of Praise* a much more precious book to me. The work they put into it came from a simple love for the Lord Jesus, plus a desire to have the best hymns possible for the Chinese Christians to sing and enjoy.

There were three hymnal project advisors: Bishop Shen Zigao, Professor Yang Yinliu, and Professor Ma Geshun. Professor Ma, choral professor at the Shanghai Conservatory of Music, was one of the first China Christians I met. His home in Shanghai was one of the first Chinese homes (in China) I ever visited. I shall not soon forget that cold December night when his lovely wife Ruth -- with help from their granddaughter-- served Jimmy Allen, Buryl Red, Ralph Tacker and myself one of the most delicious sweet soups I have ever tasted. We were even closer friends after I learned that Professor Ma had been a classmate of the brother of Grayson Tennison, a classmate of mine back in Howard Payne University.

The *Hymns of Praise* is a collection of 400 hymns. Of these, 292 are widely known in churches all over the world. Chinese either composed or adapted 102 of the hymns to Chinese tunes. Fifty-six of these were composed by Chinese Christians in recent years. At the back of the hymnal are 42 additional gospel songs and choruses.

Hymns of Praise contains hymns from the early church, Greek sacred pieces, songs from the middle ages, Latin hymns, and Martin Luther's "A Mighty Fortress is Our God." There are even two ancient Chinese hymns -- one from the *Jingjiao* (Nestorian Christianity) period (8th Century A.D.) and one from the Ming Dynasty (15th Century A.D.).

During 1981-82 more than 2200 hymns were submitted from all parts of China for consideration for use in the hymnal. Ten separate drafts of the hymn selections were made, and numerous trial performances were held in several cities before final decisions were made.

One rainy Shanghai night in September 1985, Shi Qigui and I walked from my hotel to the Community Church on Heng Shan Road. That Monday night the choir of the church was giving a sacred music concert with a large group of the Shanghai Symphony. As a rule I do not attend such affairs. My favorite music is symphony and overturns to operas -- no singers please! Just give me the full orchestra with lots of brass and drums.

95

With all the church windows open and the patter of soft rain outside, I got the best of both worlds. I heard some of the most dedicated hymns and some of the most beautiful instrumental music I had ever heard. They even sang one of my favorite Chinese anthems, "In Love He Chose Me." written by Shi Qigui. Ma Xila, younger brother of Professor Ma Geshun, led the choir. Pastor Yang Anding spoke on the importance of music to the Christian. It may sound trite, but it was a night to remember.

Of the various ways of meeting spiritual needs, none is more important than providing for the literature that inspires and informs the believers.

The regular Chinese script called *fantizi* is used all over the world but the Chinese Communist Party followed studies made years before on how to simplify written Chinese. They call the simplified *jiantizi* and it is common all over China and also used in Singapore. It has made it much easier for children to learn to read and write much faster. The New Testament, Psalms and whole Bible are published in China in *jiantizi.*

The Easter season, 1989, was celebrated with the Amity Foundation Printing Press publication of the complete Bible in the simplified script. On November 8, 1986, the Amity Press broke ground for their printing plant. The first Bibles began to come off the presses in June, 1987, and in the last week of September, 1989, their one millionth Bible was published and distributed.

Dr. Eugene A. Nida, a special consultant for the American Bible Society and the United Bible Societies, shared insights into the importance of the United Bible Societies China publishing project at the 170th annual meeting of the American Bible Society. In 1998 the 20 millionth Bible came off the press. This is one item made in China that is not in WalMart or K-Mart. They are for use in China. More on the Bible publication in the next chapter. Dr. Nida said:

Interest in the Scriptures in Mainland China is by no means restricted to church constituencies. At two different universities I was specifically asked to lecture on the Bible, and these lectures proved to be by far the most popular with students. Moreover, in one university a course on Bible content has been offered because, as one professor said, 'We know that we will never understand Western Civilization, and particularly English literature, unless our students know much more about the contents of the Bible.'

Dr. Nida went on to say, "Those who have been trying to smuggle Bibles into China have caused such Bibles to be regarded as political documents, for these smugglers have claimed that the Bible is the answer to Communism. The Scriptures are certainly not an answer to any political system. Rather, they are the answer to people's deepest longings and concerns."

Tang Shoulin, under the pen name of Tang Xing, was the editor of the 1939 Chinese edition of the devotional book, *Streams In The Desert* (compiled by Mrs. Charles Cowman). In November 1983, Tang Xing edited another daily devotional book called *Spiritual Manna (Lingcheng Mana* in Chinese) which is one of the first attempts to meet the devotional guide demand. It is an active and positive book filled with hope and victory in the crucified and resurrected Lord. Another well-received devotional book has been Wang Weifan's *Lilies of the Fields* in both English and Chinese.

On a continuing basis, the Jinling Seminary in Nanjing publishes twice a year *The Jinling Theological Review*. It covers a wide range of topics from theological discourses and Biblical studies to sermons, poems, hymns and items from seminary alumni, church leaders and local pastors. Excerpts of the *Jinling Theological Journal* were for many years translated and published each year in English by the Foundation for Theological Education in Southeast Asia. Money and interest in the project sputtered to a halt in the mid 1990s.

The Protestant church monthly, *Tian Feng* (sometimes translated as *Heavenly Breezes* in English) is edited in Shanghai by Shen Cheng'en and is distributed through the local Three-Self Committees and Christian Councils. *Tian Feng* has many overseas subscribers including Chinese-language churches of all denominations around the world. Pastor Shen and his cohorts now produce a first-class slick magazine with beautiful color photos and devotionals, articles and poetry from Christians in China. News of Western and other Asian countries are also included. (To read some translated material from the magazine log onto the Internet at the Amity News Service site: <www.pacific.net.hk/~amityhk/>)

One of the greatest publishing and distribution feats is that of getting a Bible Syllabus out quarterly to some 40,000 subscribers. This syllabus is used to help inform pastors and lay-workers and to encourage the thousands of home gatherings and Meeting Points.

About twice a year a booklet of sermons is published from the city of Hangzhou. *Sermon Collections* (Called *Jiangdao Ji* in Chinese) are sermons by pastors from around China. From reading and translating a number of these it is evident to me that the Chinese pastors and people love conservative Bible preaching.

Matthew Tang (Tang Matai) was the beloved pastor, before liberation, of the Dongshan Baptist Church in Guangzhou, Guangdong province. Afterward, when denominations were no more, he was a giant in meeting the spiritual needs of his people. Pastor Tang passed away in November 1981. He had been faithful in continuing the work the first Baptist missionaries began in his city in 1837.

Matthew Tang was a leader and a servant. He knew the suffering and uncertainty that a life given over to the total faith in God can produce. In his memory, the China Christian Council published two volumes of his sermons.

One of those sermons, the last to be written by Pastor Tang, was reprinted in the November 1984 issue of *The Bridge*. With the kind permission of Editor Deng Zhaoming I am including an adapted portion of Matthew Tang's sermon. The title is "So

Teach Us To Number Our Days." It lets us see something of a pastor's heart in today's China.

Dear friends, how the years rush by. In the blinking of an eye, we have stepped already into the last week of 1981. During the next two weeks we shall remember the joy of the time of our Savior's birth. So today, let us consider the text: "So teach us to number our days." It is a psalm written during the busiest and most anxious days of Moses' life.

As you know, at a certain point in the psalm, the composer will place a rest to allow the singer, the musician and the audience to pause and reflect and savor what has just been sung, to keep silent and await what they will hear next. This heightens their appreciation of the song. So when you read the psalms you frequently come across the word "selah." Selah indicates it is time to pause, to ponder and to wait before the Lord.

Moses was not only a religious man used by God, but a man revered as a great leader by the Israelites. He was a people's hero. He not only laid out many statutes and decrees, but drew up detailed orders of worship and ritual. He was also a poet of those ancient days. Four hundred years before the great Jewish poet David, Moses had already set down the famous 90th Psalm. Although not many of his poems have come down to us today, each one we have is significant, not only for the beauty of its rhetoric and richness of its poetry, but for its deep meaning and the profound lessons it holds for us. Therefore I want to spend some time on the psalms of Moses.

Moses' life spanned 120 years, divided into three periods. From childhood to age 40 as the son of Pharaoh's daughter; from age 40 to 80, wandering in the wilderness of Midian, a solitary shepherd, growing in spiritual ways; from age 80 to 120 God used him to lead Israel from bondage in Egypt to the banks of the Jordan

River in Canaan. It was only in the latter period of his life that his work was successful.

During this period, Moses wrote three very famous psalms which reflect his greatness. The first is in Exodus 15:1-18. It is a song of thanksgiving and praise to Yahweh. Nowhere in the psalms does he praise himself; all glory is given to God. This fact and this psalm should be studied carefully by every child of God.

The second psalm Moses wrote is in Deuteronomy 32:1-43. It was written on the eve of the conclusion of his task, it has a last testament quality. Even though Moses reached the lofty age of 120 he was spry and alert to the end, "his eye was not dim, nor his vigor abated" (Deuteronomy 34:7). To the last day he lived on earth, he spared no effort in carefully teaching the chosen people of God. This is a psalm worthy of much study, even of memorization.

The third of Moses' psalms is the one I have chosen for today. Psalm 90. It was quite possibly written when Moses was about 100 years of age. During those busy days, it appears Moses paused to number his days, and this thought becomes the central theme and heart of the psalm.

In this same spirit King David once entreated the Lord that he might know the measure of his days, to see how transient life is (Psalm 39:4)! Moses in Psalm 90:6 says, "In the morning it flourishes, and sprouts anew; towards evening it fades, and withers away." Both these great men felt that life passes in the twinkling of an eye! How precious are one's days!

Since our lives are so short and precious, how should we then use them? With the year drawing to a close, we would do well to have a summing up, an accounting. James, Our Lord's younger brother, once commented on the way some people make plans: "Today or tomorrow, we shall go to such and such a city, and spend a year there and engage in business and make a profit. You do not know what your life will be like tomorrow. You are just a vapor that appears for a little while and then vanishes away" (James 4:13-14). Human life is like the morning dew!

That is not said to discourage, but to state a fact.

I once learned a profound lesson at a memorial service for a young man. It came from a love letter he had written his fiancee while away on a trip. Besides expressing his love for her, he told of his business plans and also enclosed a precious gift, something he wanted especially to give his sweetheart. No one could have known that on the very day she received the letter and gift, he was killed in an accident far away. Human life is like the morning dew; our lives are as narrow as the palms of our hands! How dangerous it is to rely only on ourselves in all our dealings. We should listen again to James as he instructs us on how to live: "If the Lord wills, we shall live and also do this or that" (James 4:15). Let us begin today to offer our days to God for his use, doing our work according to the will and plan of God. As the apostle Paul said, "He died for all, that they who live should no longer live for themselves, but for Him who died and rose again on their behalf" (Second Corinthians 5:15).

So as the year draws to a close we need to examine what our life has been. Let us have a "selah," pause for a moment of quiet and listen to what our Lord Jesus said so long ago, "Do not lay up for yourselves treasures upon earth, where moth and rust destroy, and where thieves break in and steal. But lay up for yourselves treasures in heaven, where neither moth nor rust destroys, and where thieves do not break in or steal" (Matthew 6:19-20). God's concern is that our life is not all wrapped up in the material to the neglect of the spiritual. It is a pity that so many people work hard all their lives only for material gain and neglect the spiritual. It should come as no surprise that in the face of reality, they often find human life empty! Jesus said clearly, "Man shall not live on bread alone, but on every

101

word that proceeds out of the mouth of God" (Matthew 4:4).

God's word is truth. God's word is life. Therefore, to receive the word of God is to gain the treasure of heaven, to receive the blessing of heaven. Whoever is willing to work for God has already laid up treasure in heaven.

A Christian, standing on the foundation of Christ, should use his or her days well and build something solid and incorruptible. The Apostle Paul reminded the Christians at Corinth to build their lives on good foundations, for the day was coming when each man's work would be tested.

In the closing days of this year, we should examine our own work. Some of you may have done work that is of gold, silver or precious stones; work that passes the test and is pleasing to God. Some of you may have done work that appears to be very good and receives much praise and appreciation from spectators, but, it cannot stand the test of fire. In the twinkling of an eye, a life's work is nothing. Friends, may I ask you, have you ever examined your lives closely? We ought to ask God today to teach us to carefully number our days, so that the work we do will not be wood, hay or stubble, but gold, silver and precious stones--work that will stand the test of time and more--will pass God's test.

Finally, listen to how Paul summed up his days. He wrote to Timothy, "Be sober in all things, endure hardship, do the work of an evangelist, fulfill your ministry. For I am already being poured out as a drink offering, and the time of my departure has come. I have fought the good fight, I have finished the course, I have kept the faith; in the future there is laid up for me the crown of righteousness which the Lord, the righteous Judge, will award to me on that day; and not only to me, but also to all who have loved His appearing" (Second Timothy 4:5-8). Paul could sing such a song in his final days because he had numbered his days. He had already worked with heart and soul building a solid and incorruptible foundation that none could destroy.

Could Moses, the man of God, be any different? A faithful servant, a unique and great leader of God's people. Yet he never thought of himself as great. He knew he had nothing of which to boast. He knew if he failed as a good steward of that intrusted to him, all his days would be as nothing. So it was that at the busiest, most troublesome days of his life, he found he had to grow quiet, to ask God to teach him to number his days and to find wisdom. When he looked back through God's eyes, the experiences in the wilderness were not in vain. Though they were days of bitterness and misfortune, in his inmost self, he was filled with happiness; the beauty of the Lord came to him. Though he wandered in the Sinai for many years, years that could have appeared as wasted, and he did not cross Jordan, God's goodness and promises were fulfilled for him. In numbering his days he also numbered God's abundant grace and love. He knew he had not fought alone nor failed his Lord. He could sing his song of victory with confidence: "Let the favor of the Lord our God be upon us; And do confirm for us the work of our hands; Yes, confirm the work of our hands" (Psalm 90:17).

Dear friends, as this year draws to a close, let us all grow quiet for some moments, make a silent "selah," examine ourselves and pray, asking God to teach us to number our days and to make good use of future days to bear even more fruit, not only receiving grace from God, but in returning glory to God our Father. A-men.

The spiritual needs in the countryside are much the same as in the cities. The level of education is lower, but in some cases the peasant farmers are richer. In one country church in Zhejiang Province, the men gave many man hours of manual labor to have a church building in their village. Though they took time away from their fields and other work, they testified that, when the church was finished, God had blessed them in their own work and fields three times greater than the year before.

There is one problem in the countryside that I have not found anywhere else in the world: In many places there will be, among those attending services, as many nonbelievers and inquirers to the faith as there are Christians in attendance. This presents a problem in trying to meet the individual needs of so many who have so little knowledge of Christ. The church workers in the countryside cannot do a lot of visitation of prospective or interested believers because these come to the church! Instead of having to seek the lost lambs, the lambs are all over the corral.

Eighty per cent of the people live in a rural setting. The theology that is being born in China must take that into account -- for one of the brightest stars in the Chinese flag represents the peasants and the farmers. The other four stars must be considered in the development of a Chinese theology and ministry: the intellectuals, the workers, the military and the Party. All of these have individual spiritual needs -- needs that the emerging churches of China have the unique ability to meet.

The fruit that is being born upward through the life and work of the faithful is meeting the basic spiritual needs of the Chinese people. And the Lord is adding to their number day by day those who are being saved.

From such experiences by Chinese Christians from all walks of life can grow a theology that is as much a part of the culture as Christianity has become in American and the Western world. All different, all expressing the faith in their own way.

As Bishop Ting has said the church in China has the right to develop a Chinese church just as Americans have developed their churches and Europe and Africa have developed their churches. This takes time and the non-Chinese and even Chinese from Hong Kong, Singapore, Taiwan and the Western world need to pray for the development of a lasting and meaningful Chinese theology. It will possibly take a century to accomplish but cannot be done if Western denominations and mission boards continue to use their very foreign evangelistic methods in covert or even open ways as that is not what China Christianity needs.

The next chapter goes more into detail on "giving a cup of cold water in Jesus' name" through the Chinese Christian initiated Amity Foundation of Nanjing, China.

To help Chinese believers have more access to the Bible, Ralph Covell, long-time colleague and friend in Taiwan and the China mainland (and author of numerous books on Christianity in China), shared with me that there are now three different types of revision of the Chinese Bible in progress. One is a thorough academic effort by the United Bible Societies personnel in cooperation with mainland scholars. Another is a kind of minor correction being made by a group in Taiwan though without any consultation with traditional Bible societies. A "surface revision" is being done by the Institute of Christian Culture Studies at Renmin University.

Sources in Taiwan tell me there is an ecumenical translation being done by Catholic and Protestant translators. This will be a first for the Catholics and the Protestants have from the beginning used their own translations.

CHAPTER EIGHT

Meeting Human Needs in Today's China

"This is pure and undefiled religion in the sight of our God and Father, to visit orphans and widows in their distress, and to keep oneself unstained by the world...For just as the body without the spirit is dead, so also faith without works is dead."

--- James 1:27 and 2:26.

The Amity Foundation

From the moment it seemed possible in 1979 for Christians to come back and reclaim their churches and property in China, there was the desire to somehow let the government know that Christians could contribute to China's enormous changes toward modernization.

It was in April, 1985, that the Amity Foundation was created, not as a church institution, but to be a sister organization that would show the people how Christians care and that Christians do contribute to the re-building of the nation.

Through this non-religious and non-governmental foundation Christians could minister to needs that possibly local churches could not cope with. At the same time, foreign Christians, churches, mission boards or societies, and individuals interested in China would have a means of a legal and abiding witness to their faith in China. Since it is not direct church aid the Amity organization does not violate the three-self principle.

Amity, which is *ai de* in Chinese (two Chinese words meaning "love" and "virtue"), is a means by which the Christian message can be seen in a social ministry that involves all peoples. While the organization is still in the process of establishing priorities, relationships continue to develop with organizations inside China and around the world.

Most of the projects are in Jiangsu Province. There is a possibility of expansion as time, personnel, and money become available. Amity is a new form of Christian involvement in the Chinese society. Chinese society still looks upon Christianity as foreign and useless. That ignorant view needed to be changed. General Secretary and director of Amity, Dr. Han Wenzao, explains: "In this endeavor, Chinese Christians are joining hands with friends in China and from around the world to create an organization specifically designed to serve the humanitarian needs of all the Chinese people."

Amity's goals are basically three: First, they want to contribute to China's social development and efforts toward modernization. Second, Amity desires to make Christian involvement and participation more widely known to the Chinese people. Third, to serve as a channel for the ecumenical sharing of resources and international people-to-people relationships.

The founding Board of Directors included two former presidents of Nanjing University, Chen Yueguang and Kuang Yaming. Until her death at age 93 in November 1985, Wu Yifang, former president of Nanjing Normal University, also served on the Amity Board. Dr. Wu entered the first class of Jinling College in Nanjing in 1916. She received a Ph.D. from the University of Michigan in 1928. She was the first woman president of a China university and I had had the privilege of meeting her at a reception given for her by her students in 1982.

Other Amity founding Board members were K.H. Ting (first president of the Board); Ms. Fang Fei, Vice President of the Jiangsu Association for Friendship with Foreign Countries; Li Shoubao, General Secretary of the China YMCA; Xu Guomao, retired General Manager of the Jin Cheng Bank; Xu Rulei, Vice Director of the Center for Religious Studies, Nanjing University; and Zhao Fusan, Professor of the Graduate School of the Chinese Academy of Social Sciences; George Wu, Zhejiang Pastor Peter W. H. Tsai and Shandong seminary head, Bishop Stephen S. Y. Wang.

Dr. Eugene A. Nida, consultant to the United Bible Societies and world renown educator, said in an early Amity brochure that

"The Amity Foundation provides a creative opportunity to make an important contribution to the life of the world's largest nation. The programs are realistic and the potential is enormous."

Some of these programs have to do with teaching, Bible printing, and participation in medical and social service. Initial support of each of these projects is usually raised already in China. Following are listed some of the early efforts that Chinese Christians, through Amity, invited friends in China and abroad to join with them in undertaking. As time, money and personnel make it possible more projects will develop.

The Teacher's Project

The 1985-86 school year saw twenty-two teachers from the U.S.A., Germany, Canada and Hong Kong begin teaching English and German in colleges and universities in Fuzhou, Nanjing, Suzhou and Yangzhou under the auspices of the Amity Foundation. The teachers, sponsored by groups from abroad, all had good reports from the schools they worked with. They showed a definite concern and love for China that is sometimes lacking in foreign teachers. The Amity teachers attend church in their area and are free to invite students to attend with them. They enter into the life of their universities as far as language and interest will allow. Teachers with Amity are not missionaries. They are educators.

There were 50 teachers involved in the 1986-87 school year. By the 1988-89 school year there were more than 80 teachers relating through Amity in 50 schools of higher learning. Many of these institutions do not normally have access to native speakers of foreign languages.

Amity reduced the number of teachers during the 1989-90 school year to 64 due to the uncertainty following the Tiananmen Incident of June 4, 1989. Plans for the 1990-91 year are for almost 100 teachers in various universities, institutes and colleges in Jiangsu, Jiangxi, Zhejiang, Fujian, Shandong and Anhui provinces.

Stephen Ting (Ding Yanren), is an Associate General Secretary of Amity and director of the Teacher's Project. He received his Master's Degree from Columbia University and is a professor at Nanjing University.

The Amity Printing Project

This joint effort with the United Bible Societies to publish Bibles and other literature of service to society began in the hearts and minds of many as far back as 1983.

On November 8, 1986 ground was broken and construction begun on the site outside of the city of Nanjing in Jiangning County. The building was completed in the summer of 1987 and the printing of Bibles and the 1988 Amity calendars begun in October 1987.

None of the Bibles printed by Amity are for export. Amity could make a lot of foreign exchange by exporting Bibles but that is not their purpose. Their purpose is to make the Bible available to the whole of China.

This project meets many needs. In addition to providing Bibles and other literature for Christians, they print a wide variety of material that benefit all the people of China. As of December 1989 there had been so many orders for Bibles that there was no time or money to print anything else. Bible printing comes first, even though the need for hymnals and others books need to be met.

In 1988 the Amity Press became a Joint Project with Peter MacInnis as General Manager. The Press prints Bibles in five dialects of China including the basic Chinese Union Version of 1919. Today the Press is no longer a Joint Project and has several foreign colleagues, one formerly with the SBC IMB in Taiwan and Hong Kong, Faye Pearson.

During the Easter season of 1989 the first Chinese Bibles in the simplified script were printed. At the end of September 1989 the one millionth Bible came off the Amity presses. Up until 1988 Bibles could only be purchased at churches. A pilot project of selling the Bible through the *Xinhua* chain of bookstores proved popular but almost impossible to keep up with. The problem is keeping enough Bibles in stock. This is a problem with any popular item in Chinese markets and stores.

The pressing demand for more hymnals began to be met in the latter half of 1989 with the publication of 450,000 hymn books, including 150,000 of the old Little Flock hymnal. Only the cost of paper and time keep them from getting more hymnals and devotional materials out. The United Bible Societies raises money and promotes only the production of Bibles. Others will have to take up this challenge of providing paper for hymnals, seminary textbooks and other Christian literature. It can be done in China if all Christians, in China and abroad, will get under the burden.

The 20 millionth Bible was published in 1998 by the Amity Press.

Social Services Projects

The various social involvements of Amity are already helping to change the face of Christianity in China. The fact that Christians can participate and witness in society is becoming more widely known even to the Chinese themselves. Up until now the Christians have done little regarding social ministry.

Mr. Xu Xunfeng, one of Amity's Associate General Secretaries and for a time headed the Social Welfare Division, emphasizes work on the grassroots level, especially in rural areas. During 1989-90 Amity has brought 35 women doctors from Qinghai province to study in Nanjing. These are mostly of the nationalities, not Han people. Tibetans, Uygers and those who serve in very difficult remote areas.

Amity's experience has been that a phase-by-phase approach helps the receiving side to make better use of its own initiative and creativity, so as not to become dependent on Amity or on any Western funding agency. Another Associate General Secretary is Mr. Gu Renfa who directs Amity's liaison office. Ms. Tan Liying is an administrative assistant in the Nanjing office.

Dr. Philip L. Wickeri, on loan from the Presbyterian Church, U.S.A., was the first overseas coordinator for Amity with offices in Hong Kong. Few foreigners have studied the present and immediate past situation of Christian development in China

111

more than Wickeri. He and his wife Janice taught at Nanjing University from 1981 through 1983. Philip Wickeri had the distinct honor of being ordained to the ministry by Saint Paul's Church in Nanjing. His years of service as a lay minister and missionary are evident to the Chinese leadership. His book, *Seeking the Common Ground* (Orbis Books), a history and interpretation of the Three-Self Movement stands alone as a standard for understanding the path the Chinese Christians have traveled the last fifty years.

Joining Wickeri, and secretary Eva Lai, in the Hongkong office in 1988 were former Amity teachers Dr. Gotthard Oblau and his wife Claudia Wahrisch-Oblau of the Vereinigte Evangelische Mission of the Federal Republic of Germany. Wickeri is now on the faculty of the San Francisco Seminary but keeps close contact with China Christianity's development. Coordinating the Hong Kong office for the last few years has been Ewing "Bud" Carroll, Jr., a Methodist colleague from our Taiwan days.

A proper understanding of China's Christian history is vital to appreciating what the leaders are trying to accomplish with Amity. In the first Amity Newsletter of 1985 insight is gained in this regard: "The relationship between the missionary movement and colonialism is a widely accepted matter of historical record and still influences the way in which Christianity is perceived in China. Even in the 1950's, the statements of many individuals and organizations overseas inhibited the possibility of international Christian cooperation and social involvement. Since then there have been significant changes on all sides, and the Amity Foundation welcomes a new day in social service and international relationships."

Amity has been asked to help in funding the only Christian Middle School now in China. The Longquan Christian Church began the school in 1985. The Yangzhen (meaning "bring forth true knowledge") School has 14 teachers, eight retired teachers recruited by the church.

The Christians of China responded through the Amity initiative to give RMB 30,000. (approximately US$10,000) to the Jiangsu Artificial Limbs Factory. (RMB is short for

Renminbi, name of the *yuan*, China's monetary unit.) An additional RMB 20,000 was given for the purchase of toys and equipment needed for physically or mentally handicapped children.

According to statistics, China has about 1.8 million deaf children under the age of 14. Unfortunately deaf children are increasing at about 20,000 to 40,000 every year. Research has shown that 80 percent of the deaf still have residual hearing ability. Many can be helped if early diagnosis and rehabilitation can be undertaken.

The Amity Rehabilitation Center for Hearing Impaired Children was officially inaugurated on October 20, 1988. The Amity Foundation is cooperating in this joint effort with the Nanjing Deaf and Mute School, Hospital Number 414 and the Research Center for Special Education at Nanjing University. The aim of the center is to bring more deaf children back to the world of sound and to contribute to the pioneering work of rehabilitation for the hearing impaired.

Ms. Tan Liying, representing Amity on the Executive Committee, said twelve deaf children between the age of two to six were enrolled in the first training course from October 1988 to July 1989. Five of these children were admitted to regular primary schools after the course. The one-year program can be extended when necessary. It is hoped that the enrollment can continue to be enlarged.

Amity is funding the center with 12,000 yuan which is equivalent to nearly US$3,000. Groups and individuals from around the world and in China can have a part through giving any amount they care to. For those who might visit China the center is located on the campus of the Nanjing School for the Blind, 32 Yu Dao Jie in Nanjing.

In addition to these projects others such as Medical Lectureships for qualified physicians from abroad and exchanges among American and China hospitals and medical schools are in various stages of activity.

Chinese Christians have taken the lead in helping to develop a training program on nutrition and diet for nursery and kindergarten cooks and health care staff at the Drum Tower Hospital in Nanjing.

In the beginning Amity helped with projects of proven merit that were already under way. Now they are able to initiate worthy projects themselves as well as meet needs arising from natural disasters such as the 1988 Zhejiang province typhoon damage and the 1987 earthquake damage in southwestern Yunnan province. Amity is to be a channel of service, rather than merely being a fund-raising and banner waving entity.

Correspondence regarding any Amity project or to be on their mailing address can be addressed to:

THE AMITY FOUNDATION AMITY OVERSEAS OFFICE
#71 Han Kou Road   13/F Ultraface Building
Nanjing, China   5, Jordan Road
Zip Code 210008   Kowloon, Hong Kong
                       E-mail: amityhk@pacific.net.hk

In South China in the city of Guangzhou, Christians organized the Guangzhou Agape Social Service Center. They have a Health Care Kindergarten especially for children who are carriers of the hepatitis-B virus. In 1989 there were more than 300 applications but because of space and staff shortages they could take only 174 children. It is estimated that there are 10,000 children carriers of the hepatitis-B virus. These children cannot be enrolled in ordinary kindergartens. Without an education these children would become a serious social problem.

Dr. Lin Jingxian is Vice Principal and the staff of 17 includes a nurse and doctor. The old Church of Christ in China building and yard is used for the Agape Social Center.

In addition to the kindergarten the Center provides special recreation, exercise and physiotherapy for the elderly. Ten percent of Guangzhou's population is at retirement age. Retired doctors come regularly to give physical examinations and help the elderly without charge. They have a television set and video recorder and tape recorder for entertainment. Nearly 13,000 elderly and young people participated in the Agape Social Center's activities during 1989.

114

The director is Mr. Kao Young-chung and Rev. Lu Xixi and Mr. Xian Weixin are advisors. Mr. Guo Weixin directs the office along with secretary Grace Wang and liaison director Helen Lin.

The president of the board of directors, Pastor Zheng Baojie, said they were interested not only in making a contribution to the modernization of their country but also in providing ways of being involved in their people's daily lives. Sharing Christ by "being there." By such efforts they hope not only to expand but do an even better job.

Guangzhou is a good place for such a venture, since there are many Chinese living all over the world who have family ties with the Guangdong Province. Such overseas funding is good for both sides of the families -- those still at the old homeplace and those who have made a new home for themselves abroad.

Local and regional ventures that allow overseas Chinese and other interested people outside China to have a Christian witness--and still not infringe upon the autonomy of the local churches--is good for China and for the new Christian image.

Joint ventures are *'de riguer'* in China today -- ventures that range from oil wells to ping pong balls. Many of these ventures fail and are never carried through. Everything depends upon the local leadership --and upon outside understanding -- as to the amount of success or failure. As Christians seek ways to relate in joint ventures, the same will hold true. With the twin motives of honoring Christ and making China a better place to live, ventures such as Amity, and others, are worthy of world-wide prayer support and financial aid.

More and more First World countries are realizing that the host country should take the lead in church and Christian development. I am convinced after visiting with many China Christian leaders in various parts of the country that they are well aware of China's spiritual needs and the best ways of meeting them. The foreigner can share ideas and dreams, but no longer share the leadership.

At about the same time the Amity Foundation was being organized in China (April 1985), the leaders of the Foreign Mission Board of the Southern Baptist Convention (SBC IMB) in the United States were also seeking ways to be friends and possibly co-workers in projects that China Christians might initiate.

In order to do an even better job and enter areas closed to normal Western missionary activity the Cooperative Services International (CSI) was organized by the Foreign Mission Board (now IMB). Dr. Lewis I. Myers, Jr. was named director of CSI. Soon thereafter I became the first China Liaison Director for CSI and Southern Baptist relationships with China. Primary responsibility of a *liaison* is to keep both or all parties informed and aware of projects, need and general situation. I learned this was not always the way the IMB officials interpreted the position. (See end of this Chapter for the original CSI philosophy.)

In 1986 Jack M. Shelby, IMB field missionary, transferred from Bangkok to Hongkong as Myers' Associate for Asia. Charlie Wilson, a former Amity teacher and one of the first to go to China to study the language and make friends with the people, joined the Hong Kong office in 1989. Ms. Lena Chiu was the Administrative Assistant in the Hong Kong CSI office. Ken and Lou Ann Locke, Ron and Ina Winstead were the first China-based Education Consultants for CSI. The Lockes had formerly worked with IMB at Hong Kong Baptist University and the Winsteads transferred from Taiwan. The Lockes taught at Yan'tai University in Shandong and later in Guangxi. Winsteads taught at the old Baptist university in Shanghai and later took over my liaison work when I took early retirement in 1992.

CSI was to relate to countries that no longer needed or desired a Western missionary presence. It sounded like the wave of the future to some of us. China was the first country to give CSI an opportunity for such mutual sharing.

Missionaries of the future, no matter the place, are going to have to move more into the original New Testament mold: sharing their faith through their job and daily life. Sometimes this has been called Tent Makers-type missions but the philosophy behind CSI was deeper than that kind of iterant outreach. For the best impact upon a lost world the professional career missionary must give way to more creative approaches for

116

the coming century. Nineteenth century mission methods were never needed but it was all our pioneers knew and many good things were accomplished in getting the gospel planted overseas.

CSI, as I interpreted it, believe that the stronger the church in China becomes the more capacity she will have for ministry to her people. And the more distinctly Chinese the church becomes the more contribution she will make to the rest of the world. Working with the Amity Foundation or similar organizations in China was going to prove to be the way of the future. True for the Chinese, but still not for foreign mission boards.

In the first five years of the Amity Foundation's existence many challenging projects were undertaken. The Amity Foundation has been both misunderstood and misinterpreted by some foreign missionary groups. Dr. Han Wenzao, founding director, explains it best this way:

> Amity was initiated by Chinese Christians with the support of non-religious but socially active persons whose attitude towards religion is quite open. It is a non-government and non-church organization. In China, we call it a people's organization. It aims at the promotion of health, education and social service projects in the People's Republic of China.
>
> Organizationally speaking Amity is separate from the China Christian Council and the Three-Self Movement Committee. Funds of the Amity Foundation do not go to the support of churches.
>
> Around the time of the establishment of the Foundation, there was some misunderstanding overseas and even in parts of China that such an establishment would lead the Chinese church to depart from the Three-Self Principle.
>
> By and large these misunderstandings have been clarified. Being Chinese, we wish to take an active part in China's modernization program, because modernization is of vital importance to China's existence as an independent nation, free from the colonial

117

exploitation and domination, which hurt our country from the latter half of the nineteenth century to the first half of the twentieth century. The Chinese have been longing and struggling for generations for an independent country is not only a matter of nationalism, but it is an issue of peace and justice. If colonial exploitation and domination still remained, there would be no peace and justice to speak of.

There is another angle from which we can realize why we Chinese wish to take an active part in our modernization program. China has so big a population - - almost one-fourth of the world's population. If China fails in her modernization program, if China fails to meet the basic needs of the one-fourth of the world's population, it will cause a big problem to the world. What country could afford to feed one-fourth of the world's population?

From the first time I met with Han Wenzao I was impressed with the man. He is a bold and courageous worker yet very unassuming. I like a man who is without pretense and modest. We first talked on a cold and rainy February afternoon at the Jinling Union Seminary in Nanjing. That was in 1984, before there was an Amity or CSI. Seeing his concern and conviction that China's Christians could have a part in the New China I voiced my concern as to how the foreign Christian could relate to China in the future. "As a friend," he told me, "the foreigner can do much." The foreign Christian needs to approach the New China as a friend, not as a missionary or as one who has a foreign program for China.

After some sixteen months as the director of Amity, Han shared some random thoughts on the Amity Foundation's work:

First, I enjoy working with the Amity Foundation, because Amity provides an opportunity for Christians and non-Christians to work together. Amity is a Christian initiated, non-church, non-government organization. At present, the majority of the board members of Amity are Christians, but not all Amity board members are Christian. We even have Marxists serving on the our board. Not all Amity staff and volunteers are Christian, yet Christians and non-Christian have been working closely together. There is no discrimination in matters of religious faith.

Amity emphasizes the necessity for social change on China's terms. Priorities are established in China, by Chinese. The people of any given country are in the best position to assess the needs of their own society, and to develop the goals and methods for change which are most appropriate in their own situation. In the case of the Amity Foundation, this understanding provides a distinctive perspective for the coordination of programs and the development of relationships in China.

In Geneva in 1989 at a world-wide meeting of agencies that seek to fund genuine Non-Government Organizations (NGO) of the world, the Amity Foundation was singled out as China's only real NGO and worthy of support. The source of that unbiased professional opinion, because of the ethics involved, asked not to be quoted.

Though meeting only a few of the human needs of China the Amity Foundation is finding it better, as the old saying goes, "to light a candle, no matter how small, than to curse the darkness."

The FMB (IMB) CSI was gradually disbanded having caused more misunderstandings than necessary. Some fellow missionary colleagues saw it as a covert operation and it became such in Arab countries where Christians do not have religious freedom and covert operations are the only way if one feels it necessary to go there as a missionary.

119

THE ORIGINAL
COOPERATIVE SERVICES INTERNATIONAL
PHILOSOPHY FOR RELATIONS WITH CHINA

[Compiled April 3-4, 1986
in the Jinling Hotel, Nanjing, China
by Lewis I. Myers, Jr. and Britt Towery]

The stronger the church in China becomes the more capacity she will have for ministry to her people;

The more distinctly Chinese the church becomes the more contribution she has to make to the world.

The Cooperative Services International (CSI) seeks to be an enabler within the following guidelines:

1. Personnel are friends of China who desire to express friendship through service. They are not missionaries and do not engage in independent evangelistic activity.
2. Personnel are supportive of the Christian endeavors of China in cooperation with the China Christian Council (CCC) and the Amity Foundation.
3. Personnel seek to enhance the Christian's role as a positive contributing factor in the building of the new China. They understand and support the laws and regulations of the People's Republic of China and are committed to working with them.
4. Believing the experience of China throughout its history has uniquely qualified it for world leadership in the twenty-first century personnel seek to be available to assist Chinese Christians in sharing their experience on an international basis.

ORGANIZATIONAL STRUCTURE

Cooperative Services International is an organization created by the Foreign Mission Board of the Southern Baptist Convention, USA, for the purpose of engaging in educational,

120

health care, food production and other humanitarian projects in selected countries of the world.

The Hong Kong CSI office created for the purpose of engaging in projects in China proper. Offering services that provide personnel, consultation, liaison and funding.

Presently [Spring, 1986] CSI in China has work in the following areas:

BEIJING: One language student (Bob Freeman) Beijing Second Foreign Language Institute studying *putonghua*. Relate to Baylor University exchange program with the same institution. Projected work with the *Chinese Medical Journal*, Chen Maoxin, editor. He needs someone to help with their English editing and writing.

TIANJIN: Three staff seconded to the Management Technologies International of John Cragin.

SHANGHAI: One language student (Kim Dickey) at Fudan. Relate to Baylor's exchange program with SIME (old Baptist college). Place an English teacher at SIME.

ANHUI PROVINCE: Educational exchanges with C.K. Chang (Zhang Chunjiang) of Wuhu as liaison.

GUANGDONG PROVINCE: Relate to Bowman Gray Medical School and Guangzhou Medical University programs. Bill Swan of Macau and Tim Pinnel, liaison.

GUANGXI: Possible relationship with the Wuzhou City Hospital where Bill Wallace and SBC missionaries once worked.

HENAN PROVINCE: Several opportunities with Zhengzhou College of Aviation Management; Henan University in Kaifeng; Yellow River University project; Food processing possibilities and Carl Ryther of Waco; Baylor's nursing project connection.

HUBEI PROVINCE: Wuhan Medical needs in English with Dr. Joyce Fan (Wang Shihao) as liaison.

JIANGSU PROVINCE: Drum Tower Hospital Nutritional Science Scholarships; Drum Tower Hospital sister relationship with Baptist hospital -- possibly Memphis or one in Texas; Provincial Hospital also seeks a sister relationship; Language lab equipment and direction at the Huai Yin Teacher's College; Amity teacher (Jody Hunt) at the Agriculture Science Academy for Spring 1996; Jinling Seminary video project -- begun in 1985 by Hong Kong Baptist Mission China Program and includes other seminaries in China; theological text and library books for seminaries in Nanjing, Shanghai and Hangzhou.

LIAONING PROVINCE: Operation Understanding: one language student in Spring of 1986.

SHAAN XI PROVINCE: Operation Understanding: one language student (Jay Massy) at Xi'an Foreign Language Institute.

SHANDONG PROVINCE: Yan'tai University teachers: Eloise Cauthen for 1986-87 year; Joyce Fan asked to teach special courses April and May of 1987; Relationships explored with Yu Huang Ding Hospital; Tourist possibilities of old Baptist sites in the area; help re-open Penglai Church.

SICHUAN PROVINCE: University exchanges studied.

XINJIANG: Exchange program between August First Agriculture College and Grand Canyon College in Arizona. Arizona in Xinjiang are sister states.

YUNNAN PROVINCE: Relate to Baylor's exchange program with the University of the Nationalities in Kunming.

ZHEJIANG PROVINCE: Exchange programs suggested by C.K. Chang (Zhang Chunjiang) are with Department of Chemistry at

Zhejiang University and English Department of Zhejiang Institute of Technology.

The CSI model as outlined above no longer exisits. Today, the International Mission Board of the SBC in China uses an approach that brings reproach on the gospel and the heritage of Baptists. The publications of the IMB seldom if ever mention the work of the China Christian Council or the Amity Foundation. Leaving the impression in many of *The Commission Magazine* articles that "if SBC IMB is not doing it, it is not being done." This is not 100% the case but there is enough of this kind of reporting that is misleading to the home churches.

Integrity in any activity is vital to success and peace of mind. It is certainly true of those who take up the sacred task of sharing the life-giving gospel to others. There is no place in scripture that justifies covert mission activity. The end does not justify the means.

CHAPTER NINE

Most Frequently Asked Questions

"See to it that no one comes short of the grace of God; that no root of bitterness springing up cause trouble, and by it many be defiled."

--- Hebrews 12:15.

Behind most of the questions about Christianity in China today, there seems to be a basic mistrust of anything that a communist-directed country does. Each question seems to have an inherent disbelief that any good could come from, or even be permitted by, such a political system. I want to be neither naive nor skeptical as I try to answer just a few of the most frequently asked questions about the churches in China today.

Communist hard-liners have little understanding of the Christian faith or any religion in general. They, like all of us, have a basic mistrust of that which they do not understand. There has been injustice in the implementing of the religious policy of China. Sometimes this has been done out of ignorance, sometimes out of design, but to my knowledge none has been caused by the senior leaders of the China Christian Council.

The following is the truth as I have experienced it. None of it is secondhand gossip. None of it is a government handout. Most of these answers have come from discussions with the Chinese themselves in the Chinese language in China. I trust there has not been too much lost in the translation of ideas and concepts.

I am conscious that no foreigner can truly represent the Chinese mind and heart. I would like to try to get as close to it as I can. One day in the future a Chinese will tell the story in a way the world can understand. I pray for that day. In the meantime here are some of the questions we get from Christians in Hong Kong and other parts of the world, followed by answers that may shed a little light on the complexity of Christianity in China today.

1.   Why does a Marxist society allow religious freedom?

One fact, often overlooked by those who have never visited China nor given much thought to its 4,000 years of recorded history, is the ability of the Chinese people to adapt. Also the land of China has never know much of religious freedom. They are a people who must have invented the phrase, "to go with the flow." They know how to take a system from the outside and make it work better, or at least make it work to their advantage.

Through the centuries they have been ruled by numerous outsiders: the Mongols (Yuan dynasty); the Manchus (Qing dynasty); the Japanese; and Western nations intent on dividing China as they had Africa. Yet none of these has succeeded in changing the flow of the mighty river. As the bamboo forests bend with the typhoons, so China adapts like no nation in history has adapted. Proof of this is seen in the very age they have been able to attain as a nation.

All Marxist societies are not the same. None has begun to bend as much as the Chinese have bent in their expression of Marxism. They are saying Marx did not have the final answer. They are admitting Mao Zedong made some mistakes. Never in the history of communist nations have such wild statements been made. Such dialogue was going on in China before the dramatic changes in Poland, Hungary, Czechoslovakia, East Germany and Romania in 1989. In China such dialogue was not viewed as a threat to the Party.

China, under the leadership of Deng Xiaoping, has adapted and used whatever worked to feed and clothe the people of China in an effort to bring them into the 20th century before the 21st century arrives. A part of that adaptation is fitting into the world views of religion and human rights. Deng is smart enough to know that it is good public relations to allow freedom of religion. But there is more to it than that.

There is no agency in China today that is actually anti-religious. With all the catching up they have to do, the government and the party have little time to be promoting atheism and fighting Christians. If this simple fact could be mulled over and studied in a bit more depth, as it is by some in China, it would help outsiders a great deal as they try to understand the kind of Marxism that is emerging in China. It may not come in our lifetime, but the day is coming when the leadership of China will fully realize that when a Chinese becomes a Christian, China has a better citizen.

This will become a reality as the leadership recognizes that the China churches are Chinese. But the churches can never become fully Chinese so long as individuals and groups of Christians from the outside continue in their efforts to move Christianity in China backwards to the missionary era-- backwards to an era of church control by foreign mission boards and societies. In their efforts to keep China's churches Chinese, the Three-Self Movement, the China Christian Council and others have been sorely misunderstood. They have appeared to be anti-missionary when they are not. They are simply saying, "It is time the church of China stood up. It is time the church of China reached its own people, and to do that it must be a Chinese organized, a Chinese directed, and a Chinese financed operation. Otherwise, the bureaucrats in Beijing can rightly say that the churches depend on foreign sources; hence Christianity is foreign--and, if foreign, then 'suspect.'" China's Christians need not go through "being foreign" again.

In 1900, under the Boxers, many Chinese Christians suffered and died for being "foreign" (Nearly 100 years after Robert Morrison began the modern era of missions in China it is tragic that the majority of the people still viewed Christianity as foreign). The Chinese people saw the Chinese Christians as foreign. This has happened again and again throughout this century, reaching its height of rage in the Cultural Revolution.

Through these experiences, Chinese Christians have learned the desperate need to adapt Christianity to the local scene -- and they seek to give China's churches not just a Chinese face, but a Chinese heart as well. As the Christians of China show by deed and word that they can contribute to the modernization of China -- as well, if not better, than an atheist or a communist -- then there will be a greater respect for the gospel of Jesus Christ in that land.

This is the reason the Three-Self Movement committee stresses that the winning of China will not be done by missionaries from foreign lands, but by their own people. The churches of China must be Chinese in every aspect of their development. The words of the Apostle Paul to the Corinthian church apply to the China church of today, just as they have in every generation in every land:

> What then is Apollos? And what is Paul? Servants through whom you believed, even as the Lord gave opportunity to each one. I planted, Apollos watered, but God was causing the growth. So then neither the one who plants nor the one who waters is anything, but God who causes the growth. Now he who plants and he who waters are one; but each will receive his own reward according to his own labor. For we are God's fellow-workers; you are God's field, God's building. According to the grace of the God which was given to me, as a wise master builder I laid a foundation, and another is building upon it. But let each man be careful how he builds upon it. For no man can lay a foundation other than the one which is laid, which is Jesus Christ. (First Corinthians 3:5-11).

The missionaries laid a foundation, planted a seed, and today's China Christians are building upon that foundation and watering that seed. In the providence of God, the government of the People's Republic of China sees more wisdom in permitting such indigenous growth than in trying to cut it down. The communist has learned that persecution only flames the fires of the churches. Chinese communists are on record as admitting that they were wrong in mistreating Christians. This does not mean the communists intend to give them special privileges or treat them special. It does mean, however, that Christians will not be singled out for ridicule, nor be denied promotions. Gradually Christians and all minorities are expected to be treated equal, not be seen as a foreign religion, nor be considered a foreign-dominated form of superstition.

Wang Juzhen is a good example of this new attitude toward Chinese Christians. She is a scientist and engineer in Shanghai. She also is a Christian and a member of the Muen Church in Shanghai. Through her dedicated efforts to find a safer and better filament in the production of lighting equipment, she was selected as a model worker. At the 35th Anniversary celebration of the People's Republic of China on October 1, 1984, she was one of 17 model workers from across China to stand with Deng Xiaoping and other leaders at the Gate of Heavenly Peace in Beijing.

For one Christian to be among the 17 chosen from more than one billion people is no mean feat. It is God's hand that has done this, none other. It is saying to the non-believing government leaders that Christians can contribute to a better China. They are needed in the future if China is to succeed at modernization. It is another page of history that shows the importance of adapting to the times, to being useful to God in any circumstance and under any political system. In September of 1986 I met another Christian that had been chosen as a model worker. Wu Shouren is an engineer and one of Shanghai's Grace Church choir directors.

At a press conference in Beijing, May 19, 1984, Bishop K.H. Ting, was asked what Christianity could contribute to a socialist society. He said the Christian message of salvation and other tenets could meet the spiritual needs of people in any society, including a socialist society. He said any religion that wants to survive has to be adapted to local conditions. "Christianity in China must be rooted in Chinese soil," he added.

2. Why does the Church of China never question the Party or the government?

This question was raised by William Wan in his article "How Should We Pray For the Church in Mainland China Today?" in the *Chinese Around The World* publication of May 1985. Under a heading in his article titled, "The Three-Self

129

Movement Are the Government," Pastor Wan says: "...there is not one iota of evidence that the (Three-Self) Movement has in any way and on any occasion disagreed with the Party Policy of China."

In answering this, I would ask Mr. Wan when was it ever necessary to oppose or disagree with others in order to preach the gospel? The short ministry of our Lord Jesus on earth was packed with nothing but positive and exciting good news for all people, regardless of where they lived or how well they lived. He had plenty of Jews and Greeks around him who would have loved to hear him strike out and disagree with their Roman lords and masters. There is not the slightest hint that Jesus would have the folks of Palestine rise up and throw off the Roman yoke, or rebel against the Roman dictatorship.

His message was not "anti-Roman" and that same message today is not "anti-Communist." It is a message that is pro-faith, love, forgiveness, and reconciliation. I cannot reconcile a man to God until I can forgive him, love him, and help him see God's love through me. Such attitudes have more backing from the Bible than do those of a negative and bitter nuance. The Apostle Paul clearly shows the importance of submitting to government in Romans 13:1-7. Our Lord taught us who our neighbor was -- everyman, everywoman, boy and girl. He taught us to love all men (we don't necessarily have to like them or what they do). Paul expressed the same thing in Romans 13:8-10 and in 12:10. Christians are even to love their enemies. I take that to mean we should not give our energy and time to "anti-this-or-that" campaigns.

When the Berlin Wall fell and the Soviet Union's Communist government failed I am sure a number of American preachers had little to preach about. Their anti-Communist sermons were out of date.

It only takes a few visits with China Christians to realize they are asking questions of their government. They are in dialogue with local, provincial and national leaders in government circles and Communist Party circles. Their approaches are not as Americans would approach Washington or

130

as Nigerians would approach Lagos; their approach is Chinese and based upon an attitude of mutual respect.

The Chinese Christians do not oppose the Communist Party or their government, not only on Biblical grounds but also because the New China in which they live is so much better than the Old China (in which many of them also lived), and today they do enjoy a reasonable amount of religious freedom.

American churches of all denominations usually have an American flag in the worship center or in an activities building. Sometimes it is on a flagpole out front. In all my travels in China, I have yet to see the red and yellow five-starred flag of China anywhere in a church--nor have I ever heard a political statement, pro or con, in the churches.

3. Are there any political pastors?

A friend of mine was visiting Guangxi Province where the former Baptist church was the first church reopened in Guilin after the Cultural Revolution. In the course of the conversation about his visit to the church there, he said, "and then the political pastor came in..." I wanted to ask him about that statement. First, how did he know the pastor was a "political pastor", and what would he do, since the government wants religion, not politics in the church buildings.

A pastor friend in Shanghai said the first question visiting Hong Kong pastors ask him is, "Are you a communist?" The Shanghai pastor looked at me, almost with tears in his eyes, and continued: "We are not communist; why do they think that of us? Why is that the one question on their minds?" I wish I could explain the overwhelming fear many Christians have of communism. Could it be that our Lord knew the human heart better than anyone? He constantly said to his disciples, "Fear not, I am with you to the very end." How prone we are to forget this promise--even to the point of mistrusting our own brothers in the Lord.

There are pastors and other church leaders in China who are looking out for themselves first. They may rule like dictators or be smooth con-men in their dealings, but their behavior is no different from that of many American pastors I have known through the years. Their lack of spiritual depth or their misguided motives do not mean that they are communist or a "tool of the party".

The fact remains that today the government of China wants politics and religion separate. The message is clear: No politics in church. If a local pastor somewhere is inclined toward political science, that is his or her problem. It is not what the Three-Self committee members, nor the Religious Affairs Bureau, nor the United Front organization, nor the Communist Party, want.

Part of the reason for doubt and fear among those outside China are publications and writings that not only cast doubt on the work of the Three-Self committees, but label them as "tools of Satan himself"--as in the book published by the Taiwan Nationalist government, *The Church in Smyrna,* page 72. It is beyond logic that the China Witness Fellowship of San Francisco, California, felt that it was all right for them to use a Taiwan government press to print a book that accuses the open churches of China of being government-controlled (see page 12 of this Chinese- language book).

More of the reason for such fear of the open churches of China could be laid at the door of the Chinese Church Research Center, Ltd., of Hong Kong. In the Chinese edition of *China And The Church Today* (*Zhongguo Yu Jiaohui*) of November 1985, issue number 48, pages 8 and 9 relate an interview with an unnamed Christian in an unnamed North China location who says, "Those who worship in the Three-Self (churches) are completely under the government power, and everything they do is controlled by the government." As if that were not enough, he goes on to say, "The Three-Self organization's purpose is to destroy Christianity." The word I have translated as "destroy" is pronounced "*xiao mie*" in Chinese. It can mean eliminate, exterminate, or wipe out--a very strong word, indeed, for one Christian to use against another. If the expression is used in relation to another human being, it means "to kill". That is hardly the spirit of Christ found in the New Testament.

Jonathan Chao (Zhao Tian'en), the editor and publisher of this Hong Kong publication, seems to go out of his way in each monthly issue to deride and condemn the Three-Self Movement. Many actions they take are questioned and held up to ridicule in one form or another. A man of Chao's talent and intelligence could mean a great deal to the Kingdom of God in China if he would use his gifts to build rather than to tear down.

A pastor in central China asked me recently, "Why do they write these things about us?" I wish I had an answer. It only takes one or two rotten apples to spoil the whole crop for some folks. Because there are isolated incidents that are reported by religious dissidents, the Three-Self people always get the blame--even when the national Three-Self leadership knows nothing of the incidents being reported.

4. Is it not true that political officers check the pastor's sermons before he preaches them.

This has been answered in the affirmative by a number of publications. It is true that in the 1950s there were times and places where this took place. It is not the case now, not since the Cultural Revolution. A pastor's sermons are not checked by any political officer or even by a member of the church. One pastor in East China told how he never wrote out his sermons; there was nothing for anyone to check! I have found this true in church after church all across China. Bible teaching and religious classes are not subversive to today's China government and party leadership. If in some far off rural village, officials are checking sermons or hindering Christians -- even arresting them falsely -- such officials are out of step with Three-Self, the constitution and the Party.

5. Who pays the pastor and church staff and who repairs the newly opened churches?

I got up the courage to ask this question of a pastor in Southwest China (though it could have been considered rude and none of my business). He told me that pastors were paid from regular church offerings and that rent was paid by firms or factories still using the unopened church buildings in the area. I asked him rather pointedly, "You mean you do not receive a salary from the government or party?" He laughed and said, "The government and the party allow and tolerate religion, but they do not subsidize it!"

In cities where one or two churches have been reopened, there may be 10 or 20 other church buildings still used by people who took them over during the Cultural Revolution. Agreements, in most cases, have been worked out where these tenants pay a set fee or rent to the churches that are open in that city or county. This money is then used to renovate and keep up the buildings that have opened for worship. In some cases, it is used to pay church workers' salaries and expenses. The leaders recognize that in the long run reliance upon rent money is not best in developing Christian stewardship. This problem is being worked on. Church offerings are still the major portion of the local budgets.

6. Is the Bible published in China edited or revised in any way?

The Chinese Bible that is being printed and used in China today is the same one used in most churches in Hong Kong, Macau, Singapore, Taiwan and in Chinese churches around the world. It is called the 1919 Union Version *(heheban* or Concordia Edition). Some have dubbed it the King James Version of Chinese Bibles. The photo offset process was used to print it in China, so every page is the same as the Bible I have preached from in Taiwan, Hong Kong and Southeast Asia for 30 years.

Pastor Shen Cheng'en, editor of the national Christian monthly, *Tian Feng*, shared with me the tremendous amount of work in getting the first edition of the New Testament and the Psalms prepared and printed in the simplified script. There can be no errors. The last time it was done in China was before World War I.

For the past 30 years, China has been introducing a less complicated form of writing Chinese, popularly called *jiantizi*. Each word, or character, is made up of various strokes. To date, nearly 2,000 words have been simplified by reducing the number of strokes. It makes the learning of the written language easier and faster. More people can read and write in China today than ever before in history.

The new simplified script Bible is a great help to the younger and newer Christians who have difficulty reading the traditional or older, more complicated writing popularly called *fantizi*. The text remains unchanged. It is still the 1919 Union version, but with modern characters and punctuation.

When the Three-Self Committee was granted permission to reprint the Bible, it soon became evident there would not be enough copies to go around. A limit had to be set in some places to keep one person from buying too many Bibles, while others got none. In some churches, people signed up for their Bibles beforehand or signed their names on a list when they paid for their Bibles. The practice of requiring signatures on lists was soon dropped, however, when it became evident that a lot of people misunderstood the reason for the process. Some were not interested in having their name on a list revealing that they had purchased a Bible. It might be held against them if the government's religious policy changed or if a Cultural Revolution were to break out again.

It is for this same reason that many churches do not have a membership roll. Religion is a very personal thing in China, and they are trying to keep it that way.

7. What is the content of the pastor's sermons?

I cannot speak for the vast majority of Chinese pastors because I have not heard but about 75 to 80 different laymen/laywomen and evangelists, pastors and bishops preach. The messages I have heard, however, are very conservative in theology and biblical interpretation. I have never heard what some would call a "liberal" or "modernist" sermon in China. I have heard all the great doctrines shared by men and women

135

pastors and by young and old church workers. I had been told by some people in Hong Kong that pastors in China were forbidden to preach on our Lord's return, or on the Last Judgment, or even on the Resurrection. Such has not been the case. I have heard all of these doctrines preached with power and conviction.

Pastors are active in their communities, and more and more of them are trusted and turned to for help when social and educational problems arise. That is a social, not a political ministry.

Many messages I have heard have dealt with the abiding presence of the Lord Jesus--of the comfort of his presence. These messages are positive, hopeful and forward-looking. The Zhejiang Provincial Christian Council publishes, on a regular basis, booklets of pastors' sermons.

In September 1983, the China Christian Council published a booklet entitled *Yao Dao Wen Da,* which in English is usually called a catechism. It has 100 questions and answers on the Christian faith. Under the section on Christ, question 23, "Who is Jesus Christ?" is a good example of what the pastors are preaching today. It reads:

> Jesus Christ is the only-begotten beloved Son of God the Father, and is the Second Person of the Trinity. He shares in the divine nature and is co-equal with God. He was in the beginning with God, and was one with the Father. All things were made by him, and he is the true God and eternal life.
> (cf. John 1:1-3, 18; 10:30; Philippians 2:6; First John 5:20.)

The above translation was done by Brynmor Price, and the entire booklet of questions and answers, in English, can be obtained from the China Study Project, 35-41 Lower Marsh, London, SE1 7RL, England.

The basic content of the messages I have read and heard lift up and honor Christ. Such a lofty view of Christ could only grow out of the personal suffering endured during the Cultural

Revolution. Over tea, a pastor shared with me that the risen and reigning Christ meant more to him because the Bible verse, "My grace is sufficient for you" (II Corinthians 12:9), was not just words, not just a promise, but had become his own experience. God's presence and sufficiency became very real during the years of the pastor's separation from his family, the loss of position, and the humiliating treatment of the 1960s. When there were no places to worship together, no Bible to read, no justice--through it all there was God. Jesus kept His word. He never left them for a moment. He never forsook them.

Out of such experiences, the sermons preached in China today are anything but warmed-over homilies. They are not talks from someone's sermon outline book. They are simple messages from one heart to another, inspired by the very heart of God in the main. "It pleased God through the foolishness of the message preached to save those who believe ... we preach Christ crucified ... the power and wisdom of God." (First Corinthians 1:21-24).

8.   What is the actual structure of the Church of China?

First, it should be emphasized that the Three-Self Committee as an organization is not a church. Neither is the China Christian Council a church. These are effective channels for getting the Bible and Christian literature published, for the opening of seminaries and lay-training institutes, and for facilitating the return of church properties.

It is a misnomer to speak of a Three-Self Church. There is no such animal. The churches of China are just that--individual, separate, but cooperative bodies of believers. They seek, under the leadership of the Holy Spirit, to glorify God and witness to His reality in their individual communities. Each church is its own individual expression of faith. To meet pressing needs all around them, the churches have contextualized their faith and message. In a country church I visited in Zhejiang Province, the people shared the noon meal together. It was evident that the church building and grounds had become the vital heartbeat of that community. The Christians were relating to the whole of the life, hopes and joys of the community.

Jean Woo wrote in the July, 1985, *China Update*, an occasional newsletter of the Presbyterian Church (U.S.A.):

Many church leaders have come to the point where they feel the need for a new national structure that can determine the polity and liturgy for the church. In March 1985 a delegation went to India partly to observe the structure of the united churches there and possibly use them as models. However many in China feel that the Church in India too episcopalian. The Chinese Episcopal Church, though a strong church before liberation, had always been small, never reaching 50,000 members even at the height of its days. Surprisingly it was the former Presbyterians, Methodists and even those with the "free church" tradition who favor having bishops for the future Church in China. Their idea is to have bishops not so much as administrators but with pastoral functions as spiritual leaders. Many of the former "Little Flock" tradition have expressed the desire to join this new church. Still, there will likely be a split among those of "Little Flock" orientation because they are basically not in favor of any structure beyond the local level and many cannot tolerate the idea of ordination. But the church in China cannot wait for everyone to be ready. Already Rev. Wu Gaozi (George Wu, former Executive for the National Christian Council of China), Rev. Peter Tsai (Cai Wenhao) and Bishop Ting are working on the draft of a constitution for this new church. It will be sent to all local congregations for study, discussion and revision many times before its final adoption.

In mid-August, 1986, the Fourth National Christian Conference was held in Beijing. This was the first such meeting since 1980. Delegates from all over China (except Tibet and Taiwan) were there. They grappled with the problems of growth, revised the constitution, and brought in younger leaders.

9. What about the reports of alleged violations of religious freedom?

The latest constitution of the People's Republic of China was adopted on December 4, 1982.

Citizens of the People's Republic of China enjoy freedom of religious belief. No state organ, public organization or individual may compel citizens to believe in, or not to believe in, any religion; nor may they discriminate against citizens who believe in, or do not believe in, any religion. The state protects normal religious activities. No one may make use of religion to engage in activities that disrupt public order, impair the health of citizens or interfere with the educational system of the state. Religious bodies and religious affairs are not subject to any foreign domination.

Since this document was issued, there have been violations of its intent and spirit. One of the most unfortunate aspects of this is so few local government officials ever heard of religious freedom. Hence there are a lot of unjust acts toward religious people that come completely from ignorance. Others do it from spite alone. Claims of unjust treatment are not confined to Christians, but to other religious faiths and to citizens with no faith as well.

Two areas of China with a large number of peasant Christians, Zhejiang and Henan Provinces, have also reported the most disturbances relative to freedom of worship and freedom of religion. Most of the Christians arrested in these areas in 1982-83 were members or former members of the Assembly, or the "little flock" congregations. "Little flock" people are very independent. They do not believe in special Christmas celebrations, the wearing of makeup, or in the ordaining of pastors--to mention a few of their convictions. Some of these, and some from a similar but different group called the True Jesus Church, began in public to shout and worship in a manner not unlike the "holy rollers" who used to meet down on Third Street and Brady Avenue in my hometown in Brownwood, Texas. As a boy, I considered this an excessive form of worship. "Whatever turns you on," a friend once said. The years have taught me a little about this type of worship, and I conclude that it appears to appeal to more simple folks in more simple surroundings. Such good and simple people are easily led or misled. My use of the word "simple" here means not guileful nor deceitful, but sincere in the extreme.

Having spent some time in the villages and fields along the Yellow River in Henan Province, the cradle of Chinese society, and having spent some time in villages south of the Qiantang River in Zhejiang Province, I can say they are the warmest, most guileless, sincere and "simple" people I have ever had the joy to meet. I can see how easily they could be misled. Some have been misled. The shouting alone causes concern in the minds of non-believing communist cadres whose job it is to keep the peace, but when the noise even causes physical violence among the brethren, the cadres must step in.

What is it about facets of the Christian faith that seem to lead to violence? It will remain an enigma for me, I suppose, because my simple brain cannot equate violence with any part of the ministry our Lord lived, taught, and urged upon his followers. Yet violence is tied to the term "Christian". Every day the Chinese reads in his newspaper of the war in Lebanon between the "Moslems" and the "Christians" or the "Catholics" and the "Protestants" in Ireland. Most never stop to realize the terms here are basically political and not religious.

Although I do not recall anyone in Brownwood going to jail after a holy-roller meeting, it does happen in China. To the authorities, such outbursts are an abuse of religious freedom. To the authorities, such holy-roller type outbursts are an abuse of religious freedom. Part of the tragedy is the outside aid and encouragement given to such rural Christians by well-meaning people in the West.

I asked a Christian about this in Henan one day. His reply was interesting. He said he stayed away from the "yellers" or "shouters", as these people have come to be known in English. He knew they had numbers of smuggled Bibles from Hong Kong--Bibles he said that were different from our Bible. He was speaking of some of the new translations that have come out in Hong Kong in recent years. The difference in Bibles had caused problems. A new believer who has read only the new translation thought all other Bibles were wrong. It reminded me of the controversy that erupted in America when the Revised Standard Version of the Bible was printed in 1952. Pastors and Christians actually burned what they called the "Reviled Standard Version" and thought they were doing God a favor by ridding the blessed earth of a plague. Now the same attitudes crop up in China as various new, and sometimes poorly translated, versions of the Bible appear.

My Henan friend continued: "There are Christians in special work camps and in prisons. Some of these are there unjustly. Some are there because they spoke out against the government or the party. They should know not to do that in public!"

While I was talking with some laymen in Zhejiang Province, we got around to the problem of alleged violations of religious freedom. "We really do not know of any personally," said one of the men, who appeared to me to be a retired factory worker. One difficulty I had in talking with these men was that I had to listen with all my ability, for the Zhejiang Chinese spoken language has a whang and flavor all its own. It is not like anything I have heard elsewhere, nor is it like anything I have seen in any language book--but it is expressive.

"But do you think it happens?" I asked them.

"Yes," one said, after a pause.

I was able to get an instance from the conversation that followed. Over in the next province, Jiangxi, the Religious Affairs officials in one town decided the Christians--and especially their leaders-- needed to be reminded who was in charge. So they arrested the pastor. This was in 1984. The church members were at a loss as to what to do. Then it was decided to use legal means to get the pastor out of jail and back in his pulpit.

They took the grievance to their Residential Area Committee. From there it went through channels until the pastor was released. The most exciting part of the story was the acknowledgment by the Religious Affairs officials that they had acted in ignorance of the law. They had not known what the constitution said about freedom of religion.

Such ignorance of the religious laws abound in many areas of China. Unfortunately, most cases do not end as happily as this one. The government has a problem educating the entire nation on all the new laws, not just the ones dealing with religious matters. The *China Daily* of November 14, 1985, reported that efforts were being made toward a public education campaign throughout China to popularize elementary knowledge of the legal system among all the citizens within the next five years. Minister of Justice Zou Yu said that a priority would be given to cadres, particularly those in leading positions, and to youngsters.

In many Christian publications, the Three-Self Movement leaders have been blamed for putting Christians in jail. Knowing some of these men personally, I find this very difficult to believe. It would be totally out of character with all I have witnessed for over four years. I asked a Christian university professor, who was on his way from China to teach a semester in the United States, if Three-Self Committees put people in jail. Professor C.K. Chang (Zhang Chunjiang) almost came up out of his chair. He said, "Three-Self putting Christians in jail! Three-Self is doing all it can to get people out of jail!" Professor Chang is a teacher of sociology and head of the English Department of the Anhui Normal University in Wuhu, on the Changjiang (Yangzi River) in Anhui Province. He has no official or unofficial ties to any Three-Self committees on the local or national level. It was his first trip to Hong Kong in 45 years, and he said he hoped such lies as this were not common in Hong Kong. I did not have the heart to tell him that many Christians in Hong Kong believed Three-Self to be completely controlled by the Chinese Communist Party.

Pastor Han Chongyi of Kaifeng, in Henan Province, is an example of one who suffered for his faith during the 1950s. When the missionaries left, he took on their work of running a hospital in Zhengzhou as well as the job of seeing after schools in Kaifeng -- all in addition to handling his pastoral duties. When the Chinese entered the Korean War, America was the number one enemy. Anyone with any relationship to Americans, past or present, was considered a risk. It was a panic very similar to California's anti-Japanese sentiment after Japan bombed Pearl Harbor in 1941.

Even other Christians condemned Pastor Han. He spent seven years without justice. He did not tell me of any of this. Instead, he sat in his bedroom that cold February morning in 1984 (Pastor Han died the fall of 1985) describing the wonderful things God had done in recent years--how the church was full and, even more wonderful, how there were groups meeting all over the county in homes and courtyards, seeking to know and follow the Lord.

He had no ill feelings for his accusers, his government, or the party. He had grown spiritually beyond such things. He was a living example of what Jesus told his disciples to be: forgiving, loving and reconciled to God and man. These are the weightier matters of the law Jesus spoke about. Yes, there is still injustice in China, just as there is in most parts of the world where man lives, and the believer either grows stronger through the trial or not. The victory that overcomes this unfair world is having the mind of Christ--forgiving those who sin against us, just as the Father has forgiven us. "Be kind to one another, tenderhearted, forgiving each other, just as God in Christ also has forgiven you." (Ephesians 4:32).

10. Why are short-wave broadcasts not welcomed?

No one likes to feel they are a target. The use of the term "target groups" by the Southern Baptist IMB is unfortunate. A world-wide Chinese broadcast for Chinese around the world would be good. But to target a certain group is to demean the gospel and the people.

There are two basic reasons that the China Christian leadership do not welcome these broadcasts from overseas. The first is because they do come from foreign soil. Such broadcasts aimed at China's masses misleads the government and party people into thinking that China's Christians still rely on foreigners and it makes it more difficult to shake the foreign image.

Second, most of what is broadcast does not relate well in terms of the people's daily lives. Even if broadcast by overseas Chinese the flavor is still foreign to the New China.

Jesus identified with the people long before he ever preached. The non-China born person would do well to spend more time getting to know China than trying to preach them into the Kingdom. The Christian growth rate in China has doubled the birth rate for years. Few countries in the world are doing that. The Christian life-style in China has spoken to the masses and the churches of China are growing faster than any body of believers on earth.

I have personally talked with some of these broadcasters. For the most part they are very dedicated people. I have asked them to include China church addresses in their programs. In this way they could help their listeners find a church home. They could not see their way clear to do that. Their only reason was the old cliché: "The Three-Self 'churches' are too liberal." It is unfortunate there are mass media specialists beaming Christian programs to China who do not know the market any better than that.

Such an attitude toward fellow Christians has torn apart many a fellowship, even destroyed churches and denominations. Christians of all denominations could use a dose of "mutual respect" the Christians in China have discovered and are trying to put into practical daily experience.

Everytime I visit with a Chinese Christian I am impressed with their humility and openness to me. They do not try to tell me how to live my Christian life. They respect my faith and my religious views.

11. What about the Falungong?

The clampdown by the Communist government in China in 1999 of the Falungong has not been perceived in China as it has in many of the news releases in the West.

The Falungong sect activities do hinder the work of the Protestant and Catholic churches in China. Communist officials cannot tell the difference and often innocent people suffer. The Falungong resemble many heretical Christian sects. Some Christians are like the Falungong that claim practicing a particular style of *qigong* will avert the end-time catastrophe. Some Christian heresies require their followers to stop working and await the end of the world.

Li Hongzhi, the leader of the Falungong sect, is not a positive force in society. He is negative to an extreme and moral and ethical values Christians hold dear are brought into question through the activities of such men and movements.

The movement is so grass-roots in nature that it has caused the Communist Party leaders to watch it very carefully for they are constantly fearful of being toppled from their perch of power. Chinese empires of the past have vanished due to just this type of superstitution and ignorant zeal. The persecution of the Falungong should not be considered as anything more than more political repression and is not against religious freedom.

12. How can foreign Christians and mission organizations help evangelize China?

The answer to this begins with respecting the China Christian Council leadership that has the responsibility of taking the gospel to their own people first.   There has been a tremendous growth in the number of Christians and churches the last two decades. This has been a spontaneous movement of the Holy Spirit.

The one restriction placed upon all religions of China is that they will not be dependent upon or directed by any foreign influence.   The Three-Self Movement Committee has accomplished their goal of making the churches self-propagating, self-supporting and self-governing.   In 1988 the

China Christian Council began what has been called the "San Hao" approach. (A slogan stressing doing the three principles much better.) The emphasis has shifted from these simple three principles to doing them well. The effort now is to do a better job of evangelism (self-propagation), stewardship training (self-support) and church administration (self-governing).

Those in responsible positions in China's churches suggest the foreign Christian help in the following ways:

(1.) Encouragement through prayer support. This book is filled with people, places and projects which Christians, around the world, can lift up in prayer on a regular basis. Enter into a quiet place and intercede for the peoples of China, Asia and the world. More than half the world's population are just a stone's throw away from Singapore.

(2.) Encouragement given through actually putting into practice the mutual respect your fellow-believers deserve. Approach ministry with more of an attitude of forgiveness than judgment. The China pastors have had to do this. On all levels there are pastors and church workers that are not cooperative even within the China Christian Council. They are a long way from the harmony that most want in Christ. The point is they are working at it; they are not resigned to second best--our Lord prayed that we might be one.

When you go among a people learn as much of their language as possible. Study and appreciate both their ancient and modern customs and traditions. Seek to understand their society, religions, churches and government first. If what you have to say is relevant you will have your opportunity.

(3.) For those with a missionary call I urge you to learn the joy of servanthood. The New China offers foreigners the opportunity of being Christian servants but not Christian superintendents. Any burden or call a foreign Christian has toward China should be channeled through the Chinese national Christian leadership. They know their churches, people and society far better than the foreigner. China does not need the "professional" foreign missionary. They do desire Christian

146

friends and those who will walk along side them in the challenge they face.

I have heard it said by a Southern Baptist mission board official that their missionaries would not be "held hostage by any national Christian group." Such arrogance should have died out with the Boxer Rebellion. Any organization that tries to reintroduce the 19th century foreign mission approach is not only turning back the clock but showing a grave disregard for the approach the Holy Spirit has taken in China over the last 50 years.

(4.) Teach English in China mainland schools. There is more on this subject in this book's Afterword. There are many groups sending English as a Second Language (ESL) trained teachers to China. This can be arranged through the Cooperative Baptist Fellowship (CBF) for those interested in that channel of ministry. For more information regarding teaching English in China for a year or just a few weeks in the summer, contact Ron and Ina Winstead with the CBF in China. As of the fall of 1999 Dr. and Mrs. Winstead are teaching at the Guangxi University in Nanning, Guangxi province, PRC. See Chapter Eleven for the CBF address.

(5.) Witness through the auspices of the Amity Foundation, Nanjing, China. The Amity Foundation also provides opportunities for teaching English, Japanese, German and other languages in China schools. Christian caring and witness is possible through this organization in a number of exciting ways. For more on the Amity Foundation see Chapter 8.

(6.) Direct gifts can be made to the <u>Fund for Chinese Theological Education</u> the following ways:

Checks or designated gifts may be sent to either the:

China Christian Council,   or   Tao Foundation
169 Yuan Ming Yuan Road   P.O. Box 656
Shanghai, China 200002   Hewitt, TX 76643
                              USA
                              bet@laotao.org

or

China Connections
Kathy Call, Executive Director
458 South Pasadena Avenue
Pasadena, CA 91105

12. What are the prospects for the future of the Christian ministry in today's China?

Bishop K. H. Ting's answer to this question is one of the best I have heard. In 1985 he said:

> I can foresee that pastoral care, theological strengthening and the evangelistic efforts of China Christians will be put on a healthier basis [in the future]. This will be to the benefit of both our country and our church.

This reminds me of what the Baptist pioneer missionary to Burma, Adoniram Judson (1788-1850), is supposed to have said after suffering setback after setback. He was asked what he thought of the future prospects in Burma for the Christian message. His answer: "The future is as bright as the promises of God."

CHAPTER TEN

Twenty Years' Celebrations

*"The Lord is the portion of my inheritance
and my cup; Thou dost support my lot. The lines
have fallen to me in pleasant places Indeed, my
heritage is beautiful to me."*
--- Psalm 16:5-6

On September 11, 1999, the Christians of Shanghai gathered in the downtown Huangpu Gymnasium for a service of celebration and worship commemorating the 20-year anniversary of the re-opening of the churches in Shanghai.

Thirteen church choirs, with a 1,000 voices, representing the larger churches of Shanghai and the The East China (Huadong) Theological Seminary led the congregation in singing. As 1979 dawned there was not one Christian church open in Shanghai. Now, twenty years later there are 129 churches (86 organized churches and 43 meeting points), representing at least 150,000 members, in the city and suburbs.

More than 60 of these Shanghai area churches have been built since 1980. The East China Seminary serves not only the Shanghai Municipality, but also the four provinces of Shandong, Zhejiang, Fujian and Jiangxi.

Lynn Yarbrough, a Baptist English teacher near Nanjing, was present and wrote:

> The city's ordained pastors, minus some elderly and ailing ones, were seated behind the head tables in two rows. The program consisted mostly of music. The choirs each presented a selection in groups of four or five, interspersed with various other program elements, including congregational singing, short speeches honoring the 20th anniversary of the reopening, and the 50th anniversary of the People's Republic of China. This was followed by scripture readings and a sermon.

151

The choir music was very good. Generally, Chinese church choirs are good. Community Church Pastor Shi Qigui (whom I claim as *my* pastor for I worshipped in the Muen Church, where he was then pastor, when I taught in Shanghai) preached the sermon from Psalms 16:5-6.

After the program, Kim and John Strong and I went to Pastor Shi's home to visit and enjoy a meal with Pastor Shi and his wife Fan Peilan. It was a time of reunion for Kim, who lived two years in Shanghai studying Chinese at Fudan University. She had been very close to the Muen Church people.

How well I remember Shi Qigui. If you have read this far in the book you know of my feelings for this my "elder brother." He always held it over me when he learned he was older by four months. Since that is the case, he lets me know I should follow his lead and wisdom in all things! Following Shi Qigui is a pleasure. His humor and spirit of love and concern for China and all who pass his way made a great impression on my life.

It was May, 1982, when we first had tea together. The four of us, his wife Fan Peilan and my wife Jody sat in the parlor of the Muen Church (formerly the Moore Memorial Methodist Church, built in the late 1920s, organized in the 1870s). Pastor Shi is a home-made musician and composer in addition to being a dynamic preacher.

The sermon was powerful. The Scripture was taken from Psalm 16:5-6, which begins with: "Lord, you have assigned me my portion and my cup,..." forcefully made his point that it was in Shanghai that God had placed them and it was in Shanghai that they would minister. These are the circumstances in which they find themselves and they would not look longingly to other environments nor complain about their circumstances, but serve faithfully in the place where God had placed them.

When outsiders ask how Chinese Christians can work within the constraints of their situation, they reply that this is the place of their assignment and it is not their place to change the environment or to kick against those pricks, but to work creatively and faithfully within the framework that is their generation and their lot.

Lynn then told of the lovely time she and Kim and John had following the service. They went back to the Shi's apartment for lunch. In her letter I would be remiss if I did not share this with you for it is one of the few such impressions we have received regarding our helping the SBC relate to the CCC for the first time since 1949 when the missionaries left China. Lynn writes:

> I'll add a brief postscript to let you know that I do remember it was under your tutelage that I first came to China in 1987. Jody, I remember your taking us on an informal tour around in the neighborhood on Sunday afternoon of our first day in China, in Shanghai, and how fascinated I was and how evident it was that you were familiar with being there and at home. Britt, I remember your repeated teaching on the situation of the church in China and how foreigners should relate in a way to allow the Chinese to develop their own churches and how we should be supportive and encouraging but not ourselves "do church."

> While that path was a painful one for you all and others, and has been uncomfortable for some of us in later times, I still agree that this is the correct course and I will say again, "thank you" that because of your teaching and leadership I was able to be in the twentieth anniversary meeting; to know many of the leaders on the program and in the audience, and a valued a friend like Shi Qigui in his small, crowded study, a privilege I count as a dear treasure and grace gift from God.

Lynn worked for the Convention-wide WMU when she and Catherine Allen toured with us the Shandong peninsula seeking out locals where pioneer missionary Lottie Moon lived and worked. Allen then arranged excellent tours of the area to inspire the WMU ladies of what God had done in China. But to me I was impressed that they took the opportunity to show what

God is doing now in China through the efforts of the China Christian Council.

After 100 years of Baptist mission work in China (1836-1936) there were 214 SBC missionaries in China -- half the world-wide force. Thirty eight percent of them were women. There were 203 churches with 41,357 members. When Jody and I went to Taiwan in 1957 there were about 1200 SBC missionaries world-wide. Today there are more than 4,000 around the world.

God has blessed the ministry of SBC missionaries and yet only the hem of the garment has been touched. There is yet much to be done. And in the future much of that work must be done in cooperation, as never before, with the local Christian leadership in every country. It is a must for any relationship with the China mainland churches and believers.

China has shown in the last twenty years to be capable of carrying on the work the missionaries began. Not only being "capable" but of reaching their own people for Christ in new and inspiring ways. One day there will be a Chinese theology and it will add much to the other indigenous. mostly Western theologies that have developed throughout Christian history the last 2,000 years. An example can be found in the report of Ewing W. "Bud" Carroll, Jr., a Methodist missionary colleague we knew in Taiwan and Hong Kong.

Rev. Carroll wrote in 1999 about a interesting rural church on the outskirts of Nanjing, the capital of Jiangsu Province. Bud and his wife have spent most of their lives in Asia and today coordinate the Overseas Office of the Amity Foundation in Hong Kong.

This rural church began as a small prayer group and developed into a thriving and growing congregation. This has been the growth-experience in many areas of China the past ten years. Rev. Carroll gave the following first-hand report:

> In the early 1990s, three elderly women began meeting for prayer and Bible study in Tang Shan Township, some thirty kilometers east of Nanjing, Jiangsu Province. Ms.Tang Chuiyin was one of the

three. Twelve years ago, she suffered serious head injuries in an automobile accident. For weeks her neck was "frozen" and Grandma Tang could hardly move. During that time a nephew encouraged her to read the Bible. Not yet a Christian, she was soon struck by the countless passages which revealed a God who had profound love for all of creation, including Grandma Tang!

As she continued to read and reflect on various Bible passages, Grandma Tang's body began to heal. When asked, "Why did you become a Christian?" she replied: "I learned through reading the Bible that there is a God who loves and cares for all of us." She soon began attending a small house gathering and, by the end of the year, was baptized. Now age 72, Grandma Tang is unapologetic about her enthusiasm for Christ and the church. Nearly every spoken phrase is prefaced with "Praise God!" Her smallish, wrinkled fingers are equally enthusiastic as she firmly clasps the hands of each new friend. It is difficult to imagine this same woman was totally incapacitated only a few years ago.

The original gathering of three women soon began to mushroom. The growing number of participants at weekly prayer and Bible study sessions led to the group's purchasing an old house for worship and other meetings. However, they soon outgrew this facility and began making plans to build a new church hall and an adjacent multi-purpose building.

Bud Carroll continued:

Now the church is grappling with the consequences of China's rapid urbanization. It seems Grandma Tang and other believers began to canvass the greater Nanjing area, asking existing churches to donate or loan funds for the construction of a new church building. Many of the Tang Shan congregation also donated or loaned money for construction work. While hiring an outside company to do the major work, individual believers also volunteered their time and labor.

The Tang Shan Protestant Church is one of some 300 churches in Jiangsu Province. There are 800,000 Christians in the province, nearly 98% living in rural areas. About 70-80 Tang Shan believers gather every Friday afternoon for Bible study. Some 20-30 meet on Saturday afternoons for prayer. When asked how many people attend the regular Sunday morning worship service, Grandma Tang was somewhat embarrassed to reply, "Oh, only 800-1,000!"

Grandma Tang's enthusiasm has spread not only across her own village but within her own family. For several years her husband, a retired farmer, has regularly traveled to Nanjing by bus to purchase Bibles and hymnals for those without a copy. He spends his own time and money doing this and sells them for the same price he paid. On occasion, when he finds someone unable to afford the price, about US$1.40 per Bible, he simply notes, "Oh, you can pay me next time."

The Tang Shan church sits on a site overlooking rice paddies and vegetable gardens. However, in recent years the city of Nanjing has begun to stretch in all directions. Now, less than two hundred meters from the Tang Shan church, there is a massive apartment complex providing private housing for several hundred families.   Tang Shan may still be a rural church in history and mindset, but it now faces the dual opportunity and challenge of how to share God's love with the steady stream of "city folk" now moving into the area.

There is no way of knowing how many Christians now live in China. Records and rolls are not as important to them as in American churches. Through the years the people have learned to be careful what they put their name to. Political movements have so devastated the population spiritually and materially throughout the 20th century. What is legal today may not be legal tomorrow. Though this ancient trait of China is changing, it is still in evidence.

Just east of the church Rev. Carroll wrote about is the city of Suzhou (spelled in English in olden times as Soo Chow or Suchow -- though the Chinese name has been the same for centuries). It is one of China's most developed areas. In recent years there has been a great upsurge in the number of Christian believers in Suzhou. Out of a population of six million people, 50,000 are now registered Protestant Christians. In the past, only a handful of believers gathered for worship, often traveling long distances in order to meet. Today (1999), 44 churches and meeting points serve believers' needs in the ancient Suzhou.

In the mid-1980s wife Jody and two Hong Kong Baptist Theological Seminary professors, Dr. Jeffery Sharp and Dr. Jerry Moye, stopped for lunch in Suzhou. Pastor Bao Guping and some deacons took us to lunch along the canal. Rev. Bao, now 85 years old, loved to tell of the opening in 1979 of the Apostle's church at the end of the Cultural Revolution. He told us, "It was on April 6th, Easter. And everybody was crying during the service..."

Christianity in Suzhou and many of the eastern coastal cities was planted by Western missionaries. in the mid-19th century. Southern Baptists began work in Shanghai in 1847 but by-passed Suzhou and began a church in Zhenjiang also on the Yangzi River. It was in the early 20th century that Baptists began a church and school in Suzhou. Blanche Groves, a 1916 graduate of Baylor University, did some good work with men like pioneer pastor Feng, father of Feng Jiasheng, of the Baptist Hujiang University in Shanghai.

In addition to Baptists, the Catholic Jesuits, Methodists and other Protestant denominations arrived in Suzhou to share the faith. In 1966, on the eve of the Cultural Revolution, 14 Protestant churches and a number of Catholic churches had been established within the city. While some of these churches were destroyed during the "Ten Years Of Chaos," the majority remained intact. Not all of these buildings are being used for worship purposes today. Recovery of former church property continues to be one of the most urgent tasks for Protestant and Catholic churches in China.

Today's China churches have a chronic shortage of workers. As a result, one of the duties of urban pastors is regular visits to outlying meeting points and churches. Today, the Suzhou area has six young seminary graduates and five older pastors, which is a good number when compared with more remote areas.

One of the most pleasing aspects in many parts of China is the good relationship between Catholic and Protestant churches. This is not always true, as many Catholic believers that still look to the Pope in Rome must meet in secret. The government demands that Protestants and Catholics must not rely or have ties to foreign entities. This is easier for Protestants but a difficulty for many Catholics.

So, in a sense there are two Catholic Churches in China. One that still clings to Rome and one that is more Chinese and open. It is unfortunate that Rome is and has always been a more political religion. With its formal ties with Taiwan come more problems for China mainland Catholics.

An example of dis-information Christians outside of China constantly receive is that there are 65 or 90 million ProtestantIn Protestant Christians in China.

Is this figure accurate? Many who have worked on Protestant church statistics in China for many years can find no evidence of such large numbers of believers. My own estimate is just that, an estimate: twenty million. There is no basis for that in real hard facts. But neither are there any for those who publish as fact such high numbers.

Where does the figure "65 million" come from?

This figure was originally published by the Chinese Church Research Centre (CCRC) in Hongkong. According to director, Jonathan Chao (Zhao Tian'en), this high figure is based on a secret Chinese government report on the growth of Protestant Christianity within the country. CCRC has never published a copy of this document, and there has been no independent confirmation of its existence.

Lets take a moment to look at the real situation of "numbers" and see if the truth might be found somewhere in facts, rather than in an agenda to show up the Communist leaders.

First, government registration for places of worship only became compulsory under the "Regulations Concerning Places Of Religious Worship," which were passed in January 1994. I spoke with Bishop K. H. Ting on this in Nanjing in the summer of that year. He acknowledged that prior to this, government registration of churches existed in only a few parts of China. The registration process under the new law has started slowly, therefore there are many congregations that are still not registered with the government, even though they are part of the China Christian Council (CCC).

Second, the China Christian Council and provincial and local Christian Councils see themselves as an umbrella and support organization for all Protestant congregations in China. They organize the training of lay leaders and pastoral workers, the printing and distribution of the Bible and Christian literature, and help congregations in their dealings with local governments. In some areas, though, there are tensions between local churches and the local Christian Council, and some local churches prefer to remain separate from the local China Christian Council. But in most places, congregations, whether in or outside of the local CCC network, know of one another. To speak of secret "underground" churches in China is inaccurate: Even those called "underground churches" in the foreign press reports ususally function openly.

Third, the vast majority of all Christians in China could be called "evangelical," including provincial and national church leaders, even if they prefer not to use this label themselves.

Fourth, most of the congregations organized under the China Christian Councils on different levels are meeting in homes or meeting points. The CCC counts only about 8,000 churches in China, but tens of thousands of meeting points which may be private homes or simple halls where believers gather for worship.

In my research and "counting" I include all Christians in China, whether they worship in church-like buildings or homes, whether their congregations are part of a China Christian Council or not. (The CCC's goal is to protect the rights of all Christian groups in China to practice their faith freely, including their right not to participate in the Three-Self Movement.) But as the large majority of congregations do not have membership lists, all figures can only be estimates.

Finally, the question comes: "Who should be counted as a Chinese Christian?" Due to the lack of ordained pastors, in many rural areas less than 50% of the regular churchgoers are baptized.

Should those who have not been baptized be counted? Similarly, there are many groups who use the name Christian but have limited understanding of the Christian faith, such as those who have only heard that prayer in the name of Jesus heals the sick. Should they be counted as Christians, or should one wait until they have a better knowledge of what Christian faith entails? Such problems of definition mean that any statisticsmust be used with care.

Some foreign observers have suggested that the provincial Christian Councils deliberately give very low numbers of Christians, because they are afraid of trouble with the government.

The provincial CCC certainly tend to make conservative estimates. Why should they be interested in inflating their figures? On the other hand, I suspect that foreign groups smuggling Bibles into China or organizing radio broadcasts tend to give rather high totals for their own purposes of gaining funds to carry on their covert work.

While churches are growing fast in provinces such as Jiangsu, Zhejiang, Anhui and Henan, there is much less or even no church growth in other areas. Researchers agree that there were less than one million Christians in China in 1949, and that serious church growth did not start until the 1970s. To assume that the church in China has grown not tenfold, but sixty-fold in the last 50 years, seems rather fantastic. There has been no statistical proof for such a claim, not even a provincial breakdown by those who propagate such large figures. Rev. Claudia Oblau, who has done much research in this area and has shared much of the "numbers game" with me, says, "I believe that while our range of figures may be on the conservative side by as much as fifty percent in some cases, our figures give an order of magnitude that comes quite close to the truth."

Chapter Eleven

TEACHING IN CHINA

For anyone who has read this far in this book it is evident the book is but an introduction. It is not the final word on "things Chinese." There are hundreds of books on all aspects of China in my personal library. It would be foolish to think that even the major events of such a land could be covered in such a book as this.

This chapter does not begin to present all the possibilities the traveler, teacher or visitor to China will encounter. These are just a few personal tips gathered from those with experience in China. Some are from our years there and others are from the Chinese themselves.

Personal Reports from China Teachers

Following are insights from Kimberly and John Strong who went to China to teach English through the Presbyterian Church (U.S.A.). They are in China as partners in sharing the Gospel of Christ. They work through the Amity Foundation of Nanjing, China. This is China's only real NGO (Non-Government Organization) initiated by Christians and supported in China and the world by many churches, societies and organizations.

The Strongs both teach English conversation at a college of education in the city of Nanjing. Their first child was born in Nanjing, January 26, 2000, and the boy was named Benjamin Springfield Strong. Kim and John met as students at the Southern Baptist Theological Seminary, Louisville, Kentucky. Earlier Kim had gone to China as one of the first three Journeymen of the Southern Baptist Foreign Mission Board (FMB now International Mission Board, IMB) to study Chinese and share their faith in an open and honest manner as students.

She studied two years of Chinese at the prestigious Fudan University in Shanghai and was active in the Muen Church in the city. Afterwards she taught English in both north and south China. First is a report from John followed by Kim's remarks.

163

John Strong writes about the first days of his China experiences, December, 1999:

Upon arrival in the country, the Amity Foundation provided an orientation conference for all the newly arriving volunteers. My wife, Kim, is a veteran China volunteer, having taught English in various locales in the country already. I'm a newcomer and very much needed the benefits of Amity's orientation, which took place on the campus of the Nantong Teachers College. Nantong is a small city just north of Shanghai. We had three weeks of informative seminars about Amity, daily lessons in Mandarin Chinese, personal language tutors, seminar-style presentations on how to teach English as a foreign language, and opportunities for practice-teaching.

Besides all the activities in classrooms and conference rooms, it was a slow immersion into the culture and living conditions. Although the guest house on the college campus had nice accommodations, we were still removed from many amenities that we had been accustomed to back home. Water had to be boiled before use; some of us had hot water in the bathroom and some of us didn't, mosquitoes were more of a nuisance than we had been used to. The weather the first week was wonderful, but then the reality of what summer is *normally* like set in -- haze, heat, and humidity. We had washing machines at our disposal there, but no dryers. We all had clothes lines on little balconies outside our rooms.

The prime initial duty for me here is learning the language (Mandarin, a.k.a. Beijing dialect, a.k.a. *putonghua*, a.k.a. Standard Chinese). My favorite part of the orientation was personal language tutoring. I was paired-up with a young man named Wang Bin, a charismatic and friendly fellow with a very positive attitude and wonderful sense of humor. We became fast friends, and I was honored to receive from him a Chinese name: Wang Jun (pronounced "jwen"). Wang is the family name, Bin and Jun are given names. So now we're brothers! Chinese typically address each other using their family names, so I became accustomed to being called Strong, and I opted for calling my tutor Xiao Wang (Little Wang) as is common among friends.

One day returning from town on our way back to school, we were approached by a woman on the street who asked Wang Bin about me. Was I from America? Was I Christian? Would I like to sit and talk for a little while about the Bible? She spoke of the Gospel of Matthew, and of the Good News, of the "light that has come from God," and of her desire to arrange a meeting between the foreign Christians and her Christian friends. After our talk with the woman, Wang Bin asked me about the book of Matthew. I made an attempt to explain what the New Testament means to Christians and what the Gospels are, but even after what I thought was a simple outline, Wang Bin confessed that he could not understand most of the words I was using. This was obviously more than just a language barrier. In order to communicate with each other on a deeper level than just everyday "survival language," we have to know more than just each other's words. We know nothing of each other's experience of life, family, love, values, morality, etc. How hard it is, even in our own "hometown," to really know the people around us, and to be known by others? Pray that in the midst of my language-learning God might grant me the gift of discovering true fellowship and brotherhood with those lives I cross paths with: Western colleagues, Chinese Christians, neighbors and acquaintances.

After our encounter with the Christian lady on the street that day, there were other encounters the following Sunday at the church between a couple of Chinese women and Don Snow, our orientation leader. He told us that these women were probably part of an emerging sect called "Eastern Lightning," which promotes some pretty off-the-wall notions, primarily that the second coming of Christ has already happened and God has taken bodily form again as a woman somewhere in northern China. We have much to learn about Chinese Christianity and "Christianesque-deviations" in the country.

Kim Dickey Strong, 14-year veteran in China and new mother, writes (before the baby arrived):

The baby is an ever-popular topic with the students, and of course, we are more than happy to indulge anyone who wants to talk about our little bundle-to-be. They are all excited that the baby is due so close to the date of their big holiday--Spring Festival [Chinese New Year] -- and they are full of advice about everything I could possibly want to know. I've had good medical care here and all the doctor's reports have been glowing, so we continue to be grateful and excited as the days whiz by. . . .

Perhaps some people travel to distant lands to escape something, only to find that it travels with them and only looms larger when familiar coping mechanisms are no longer at hand. We have no idea what the whole story is, but this is a call for us all to be aware that there are people everywhere who are hurting, wounded deep within, who need evidence of God's love in their world. Please pray that our lives will be a clear sign of that love among the people here -- colleagues, students, classmates and friends -- and know that we are also praying for you, too, as you reach out to others in Jesus' name.

There was an "interesting" experience for me on the morning of September 30, 1999. The day before our Foreign Affairs Officer, Yang Qian, had called to say that the local TV station wanted to interview some local foreigners about their thoughts on the 50th anniversary celebrations [of the founding of the People's Republic of China]. Would I be willing to talk to them? I said I'd be glad to if my voice came back. I had caught cold the week before.

The next morning I didn't feel well at all, so after seeing John off to school, I watched the big flag-raising ceremony through our little breakfast nook window, and then promptly went back to bed. Ten minutes later, I heard someone tapping on our window. It was Yang Qian. Silly me thought maybe she had come by to see how I was doing, so I got up, wrapped a robe around myself (which doesn't really fit anymore!), and opened the door. Much to my shock and chagrin, she was standing there with two TV reporters and a cameraman!

It was incredibly awkward, but I finally persuaded them to give me 30 minutes to shower, get dressed, and straighten up a little. Thirty minutes later, they were back for the interview, particularly interested in the fact that we were going to have our first baby there in China. As it turns out, that's the segment that actually made it into the local broadcast. It all seems funny now, but at the time I'm pretty certain that it was nothing short of a miracle that I didn't strangle Yang Qian on the spot! God is good, and definitely does have a sense of humor!

The above accounts by Kim and John Strong are typical of many who write home about their experiences. Scores of books have been published by people about their experiences in China. One book about teaching in China that is useful is *Coming Home Crazy* by Bill Holm with an Introduction by Harrison E. Salisbury. Holm's book was published in 1989, but is still informative.

Friends of the Churches of China

Early on (late 1970s) the Presbyterian, Methodists, Anglicans and some Lutheran groups made it clear to the China Protestant leaders they wanted to be helpful in ways the Chinese thought best. This approach was well received in China. For it is evident the future relationships between Western Christians and China Christians, to be fruitful, must be based on mutual respect. The Conservative Baptist Mission Society with the able help of men like Ralph Covell have been friends with the CCC leadership almost from the beginning.

The American Baptist Church (long ago known as Northern Baptist Convention, from which the Southern Baptists withdrew in 1845) also chose to work openly with the churches of China.

During the 1970s and 1980s Southern Baptists were becoming more and more involved in a complete change of course as the Fundamentalists sought to purge the Convention of those they considered too liberal and not worthy of leadership. There are no "winners" in such denominational wars. With the fundamentalists "take-over" of the Southern Baptist Convention many of the SBC missionaries were also caught in the middle. The ultra-conservative fundamentalist began to force their form of American evangelism on the missionaries in ways that were not what the world of missions needed.

The fundamentalists were not friends of the China Protestants. They saw the churches as government-directed, too soft on Communism and needing the fundamentalists approach. They had their own agenda as I have pointed out elsewhere. An agenda of covert activity added to the suspicion the Communist cadres already had for foreign Christian bodies. A suspicion that carried over to local Chinese churches and Christians and actually made their witness more difficult.

The moderates of the SBC formed what they called The Cooperative Baptist Fellowship (CBF) and have been engaged in working with the China Christian Council and the Amity Foundation in an open and meaningful way. My successor as SBC IMB Liaison for China, Ron and Ina Winstead, soon left the IMB and have done an outstanding job teaching English in Guangxi as well as directing the CBF in a common sense open ministry in China. See Chapter Five for more on CCC-IMB controversy.

For a while Harlan Spurgeon, a colleague of ours in Taiwan and later IMB head of personnel, helped the CBF to relate to the CCC during their early years. Don and Helen McNeely are International Coordinators for Volunteers for the CBF. Their experience of having lived and worked in Mongolia, Eastern Europe, Africa and the Russian Far East prepared them for their present relationships with the CCC.

Those Baptists and others interested in becoming meaningful Friends of China Churches can look into it more by contacting the Cooperative Baptist Fellowship offices at P.O. Box 450329, Atlanta, Georgia 31145. Telephone: (770) 220-1600. Web site: <www.cbfonline.org>

Turning a corner

America and China for a generation, beginning in 1949 did not speak to each other. In 1950s America's leaders were fearful of world conquest by the Soviet Communists in Russia and the Chinese Communist in China. The American government chose not to recognize the new Communist regime on the China mainland; fought wars in Korea and Vietnam to stop what appeared at the time to be the beginning of world domination by what some called "the evil empire." Even old racist terms like "Yellow Peril" surfaced from time to time. Thus for nearly 30 years America and China did nothing to foster friendship and did everything to humiliate and oppose each other at every turn.

At the invitation of China's Premier Zhou Enlai some unusual Ping-Pong matches were held in China between American and Chinese young people. Then in 1972 President Richard Nixon visited China and a corner began to be turned in relationships between China and the USA.

President Jimmy Carter approved diplomatic relations between the two countries and by 1979 both sides could see a bit better around the corner.

It became evident to all who visited China since 1979 that the people and nation had needs in every area of life. Many were willing to help -- mainly if they could make money. Others gave of themselve out of love for the people and the message of Christian reconciliation. The road has not been smooth, but true love never is. The peoples of these two great nations need to get to know one another better and avoid more years of separation. We learn from each other through interaction.

Chinese students are coming to American in great numbers. They know a great deal more about us and our country than we do about them and their land. It is hoped more Americans will feel the "call" to China as friends. Their needs and ours are to make relationships work to the glory of God and peace among all peoples. This means new approaches to Christian mission and sharing; approaches that do not reproach, but enhance the social and spiritual welfare of China and the West.

China's Religions: A sketch of earlier days

Daoism (Taoism) is the only religion indigenous to China. The teaching of The Dao ("the way") did have competition for the hearts and minds of the people as Confucian doctrines evolved. But Confucianism is not considered a religion, but more an ethic or philosophy of life.

Years after Indian Buddhism was introduced to China and became a Chinese religion it did seriously challenge Daoism as China's primary religion.

In the sixth and seventh centuries the religion of Islam grew amazingly fast. Muslims are considered a special group today known as the Hui minority peoples.

Syrian Christians came to Xi'an as merchants and monks to China in the seventh century. They called themselves The Religion of Light and flourished for some 200 years, 635 to 845 when a great persecution broke out against all religions.

The actual arrival date in China of the Jewish faith is not known. We do know that at the end of the Babylonian Captivity not all the Jews returned to Jerusalem. Many migrated to India and eventually to central China.

It is a historic fact that the Jews built a temple in the city of Kaifeng in 1163 and rebuilt it in 1279. According to a 1489 monument this synagogue-temple was restored at least ten times. At the Birdwell Library of Southern Methodist University, Dallas, Texas, one of the Kaifeng Torahs is living proof of the Jews existence in central China. This Hebrew Torah was one of the last evidences of their presence and was purchased in the 1850s and by the 1950s had found its way to Oklahoma and later SMU.

Christianity, in its European Roman Catholic clothes or Protestant attire has had a bumpy road through the centuries.

The last time Christians of both these persuasions entered China in the early 19th century it was in an unfortunate manner. Their faith was forced upon the Chinese by war and treaty. Such a history has been a hindrance to the spreading of the Gospel of the Lord Jesus Christ.

Most Protestants in China have chosen to work with the CCC rather than return to the foreign missionary-denominational style of church. Christians in China are thankful for the missionaries who brought the message, but now it is past time for them to take the lead in reaching their own people.

There is a worthy attempt by the CCC to leave behind the western denominational approach and create Post Denominational churches. For more information visit the following Internet web sites:

The Tao Foundation and Mission Forum
<www.laotao.org/tao> <www.laotao.org/mission>

From these Internet web sites you can find "things Chinese" such as books on China and information regarding China, and links to The Amity Foundation and many web sites from or about China. For a more indepth introduction read two books by Laurance G. Thompson: *Chinese Religion* (fourth edition) and *The Chinese Way in Religion* (both Wadsworth Press). Stephen Reynolds' *The Christian Religious Tradition* is also useful as is *Religion in China Today, Policy and Practice* by Donald E. MacInnis. MacInnis' book needs to be up-dated.

BEFORE YOU GO

• **Read before you go.** Know what happened in China during this century, both politically and in society and literature. Check out the bibliography in the back of this book.

• **Appreciate the language and customs.** Be careful not to over eat (the food is wonderful -- not the semi-Chinese food served in most American Chinese restaurants).

• **Go as a friend, open to new ideas and experiences. Here are some thoughts out of the past that are good guides:**

American President **Thomas Jefferson** (1743-1826) said:
"Peace, commerce, and honest friendship
with all nations -- entangling alliances with none."

"A faithful friend is the medicine of life"
(Ecclesiastics 6:16)

John Gay (1685-1732) wrote in
'The Shepherd's Dog and the Wolf' that:
"An open foe may prove a curse,
But a pretended friend is worse."

Ralph Waldo Emerson (1803-1882) said:
"A friend may well be reckoned the masterpiece of Nature."
and "The only reward of virtue is virtue;

171

the only way to have a friend is to be one."

W.B. Yeats (1865-1939):
"Think where man's glory most begins and ends,
And say my glory was I had such friends."

• Listen

More is learned from listening than talking. Someone said God gave us two ears and one mouth, meaning we should use our ears twice as much as our mouth.

• Things to avoid

"...that rarest gift to beauty, Common Sense"
-- George Meredith (1828-1909)

POLITICS

In Lao She's play *Teahouse*, there appears on the walls of the teahouse set the sign: "Don't discuss government affairs." The play covers fifty years of China's history from empire to republic to invasion from 1895 to 1945. (For more on this great writer see my book, *Lao She, China's Master Storyteller*, published in 1999 by the Tao Foundation. His novel *Camel Xiangzi* or called *Rickshaw* in some English translations, was chosen by Chinese around the world as the best long Chinese novel of the 20th century.) His works are studied in middle schools and universities throughout China. He was also a Christian.

In Lao She's *Teahouse,* each act of the three-act play is a different era and though many things change from era to era, the reminder "Don't discuss government affairs," on the walls of the teahouse doesn't change. The sign becomes even more numerous and bigger to remind the customers of the danger of such talk.

In China this admonition is just as important at the end of this century as when the century began. There never has been a good time to talk politics in China. The Qing dynasty stopped reforms before they could be tried in 1895. Warlords never even considered the people's views about anything. The Republic of China did not react to criticism in a nice way. The People's Republic of China is also very sensitive to even tiny insignificant political views other than their own.

So the first thing to avoid in China as a visitor, tourist, teacher or worker is politics. For fifty years there has been and is the Communist Party line. Before that the Nationalist Party line and for centuries the party line of the dragon throne. Politics has never been something most Chinese discuss openly as in America. It is not in their makeup or understanding to talk as freely as do Americans about any subject under the sun.

You will find them the best students you have ever taught. They really do want to learn English and learn about your country and your experiences. When they are convinced you are a friend and a good teacher there is the great possibility they will ask you about your God and your personal spiritual journey. But you must first win their confidence and friendship. Your personal witness and life is far more powerful than all the religious tracts or books you might give them.

So plan to listen a lot and have a good time meeting some of the finest people on God's earth.

Part Two

PROVINCES
and
CHURCHES

ANHUI PROVINCE

Though the province dates back to 1662, when Jiangnan was divided into Anhui and Jiangsu Provinces, Anhui has remained a backwater province. Anhui is rich in coal and iron ore, but know for centuries as a poor area. Ma'an Shan ("horse saddle mountain"), on the Changjiang (Yangtze River), is the biggest industrial center of the province.

The northern part of the province is now covered in wheat fields and rice paddies. In the capital city of Hefei, 18 hours south of Beijing by train, the most famous artifact is the 2,000-year-old jade burial suit that is stitched with silver thread.

Up the river from Ma'an Shan is the city of Wuhu, one of the flourishing trading centers in the area. I had friends teaching English at the Wuhu Teacher's University in 1984 and visited them once. Dr. C. K. Chang (Zhang Chunjiang) was responsible for opening the school up for foreign English teachers. Years ago his cousin, Dr. Y. K. Chang was a co-worker of mine and teacher in the Taiwan Baptist Theological Seminary in Taipei. C. K. Chang was the last chaplain of Hujiang Daxue (Shanghai University), when it was a Baptist school. For over 30 years he was head of the Foreign Languages Department at the Anhui Teacher's University. During the 1985-86 school year, he was an exchange professor at Baylor University, Waco, Texas. In ill health this Baptist pioneer is a widower with little family left. He is cared for by students and former students.

In eastern Anhui province in the mid-1970s agricultural communes first began experimenting with the concept of "responsibility" farming ideas. Work that gave the peasant and man on the street an incentive to produce more and better products. It gave the people a motivating force that would change the economics of China in the 1980s. It had a quiet beginning. Such programs were thought to be inferior to the socialist ideals. But the incentives it gave to the people could not be denied. There was an increase in every crop where the method was tried. It caught the attention of government and political leaders and the responsibility "work ethic" began in Anhui, long one of China's poorest provinces.

Huang Shan, one of China's five sacred mountains, is more than just another mountain. It is a cluster of towering peaks and is a beloved place for poets and lovers of the great outdoors. It is said that, as you walk up the mountains, you pass through all four seasons of the calendar.

According to the best estimates, Anhui province is possibly fourth in the total number of Christian believers, about 800,000. Only Henan, Fujian and Zhejiang province have more, each with over one million Christians of all descriptions. Churches have reopened all over the province such as in Bangbu and Chuzhou. Pastor Zhu Shaotang of Chuzhou led his people in a publishing project that has given jobs to the people and produced 100,000 copies of the new hymnal.

Selected Anhui area church addresses:

Hefei Church
68 Suzhou Lane,
Hefei

Huainan Church

Bengbu Church
Bengbu City

BEIJING (Peking)

The capital city of the People's Republic of China sits on the same latitude as Philadelphia in the United States. Called "Peking" by foreigners, the city has been Beijing, "Northern Capital", to the Chinese for centuries except for a brief time in the early years of the Ming Dynasty (1368-1421) and the days of the Republic of China (1912-1949).

Records go back to the 12th century, B.C. when there was a state called Yan. During the Tang Dynasty (618-907 A.D.) it was named Youzhou.

The heart of Beijing is the Imperial City, the southern wall of which is the imposing Tiananmen (the Gate of Heavenly

Peace) Square. The design of the national emblem of today's China is this ancient gate, illuminated by five stars and encircled by ears of wheat and a cogwheel.

The Tiananmen Square has become even more famous since the June 4, 1989 massacre of students and citizens seeking an end to corruption in government and more democracy for China. A group of insecure government and Communist Party officials ordered the crackdown on the pretense the democracy movement was a rebellion to overthrow the government.

Many church leaders who have lived through the mistakes of the Great Leap Forward and the horrors of the Cultural Revolution felt for the students in their youthful, naive and bouyant spirit. The older generation never knew such stability as they have experienced the last ten years. It is natural many were hesistant to get too involved.

Of Beijing's population three-fifths are under the age of 30. That is about six million young people and they were saying almost to a man that change was needed.

There are possibly a dozen Protestant churches open for worship and "too many to count" Home Meeting Points providing Bible study and prayer. The Beijing Theological Seminary has been open since the spring of 1983. They began with seven students. In the fall of 1986 the Beijing Seminary merged with the Tianjin Seminary and began classes as the Yanjing Theological Seminary in the heart of the city at number 43 Dongdan Bei Da Jie. A block east and north of the Beijing Hotel. Yanjing is another ancient name for the city. During the 1990s the seminary moved out to a new campus.

Selected Beijing area church addresses:

Beijing Christian Church
Chongwenmen District
2 Hou Gou Hutong

Gangwashi Church
Xicheng District, Zip Code 100034.
57, Xisi Nan Da Jie

YMCA and Three-Self Committee, Beijing offices
21, Dongdan Bei Da Jie, Tel: 55-5086
(Former Bible Society and Rice Market Church.)

FUJIAN PROVINCE

This mountainous province on the southeast coast of China is where the ancestors of most of the present inhabitants of Taiwan came from. In 1662, Zheng Chenggong (Koxinga) drove out the Dutch from the Tainan, Taiwan area, to set up his anti-Qing Dynasty headquarters. He wanted, right up to his death, to see the Ming Dynasty reinstated to the dragon throne in Beijing. Many of Taiwan's forebearers came from the cities of Xiamen (Amoy), Quanzhou, and Fuzhou. History repeated itself when, in 1949, the Republic of China's president, Jiang Jieshi, led his defeated Nationalist forces to the island of Taiwan with plans to regroup and one day retake the China mainland.

The English word "tea" most likely came from the various Min dialects of this area that pronounced it "day". Early Arab and Portuguese traders probably borrowed the word, mispronouncing it in the process. Of all teas, Fujian tea was the most prized in the west before Indian and Ceylon teas were developed. Fuzhou is the capital city.

Fujian, after Zhejiang and Henan, may have one of the largest Christian communities in China today. A church building has been built in Pu Tian that can seat 3000 people in one service.

The Pastor of the Flower Lane Church in Fuzhou, Zheng Yugui, told me they had baptized 3,600 new converts from 1979-85. 500 churches are now open or newly built. Pastor Zheng also serves as vice-president of the Fujian Theological Seminary.

Bishop Moses Hsieh (Xue Pingxi) was the oldest active bishop in China until his death at age 91, Feb. 1, 1995. While visiting the Fujiang Seminary I visited with Bishop Hsieh and one of his former students, the late Bishop Stephen Wang (Wang Shenyin) of Jinan in Shandong Province. It was a rare treat to sit with two of China's (at that time) eight bishops.

Bishop Hsieh was of the Anglican tradition and studied in England in 1948-50. When he prepared to return to China in 1950 there were those who urged him not to leave England for the uncertainties of China. "I was needed here," he told me, "How could I run away from the flock in Fujian? How could I ignore my people in their time of need?"

Fuzhou is another of the key places where Bibles have been, and are being published. Pastor Zheng tells it best: "When we printed the Bibles in Fuzhou many of our people came and gave of their time and energy to wrap the Bibles for mailing to the churches. I can never forget seeing some of them singing hymns and praises to God as they wrapped the Bibles. Sometimes they lifted up the wrapped Bibles and praised God for his provisions and goodness in giving China, once again, the Word of God."

Selected Fujian area church addresses:

The Flower Lane Church
3, Huaxiang (Flower Lane)
Fuzhou

Christ Church
1, Yixiaqiao
Fuzhou

Chengguan Church
72 Heping Street
Fuzhou

Chengmen Tang (City Gate Church)
Chengmen Township

Putian City Church
Putian City
(Church building built in 1915, and re-opened March 9, 1986. This is the largest of 17 churches in the Putian area and seats 2500 to 3000 people. In 1988 the area had more than 35 Home Meeting Points or "house churches")

Nanjie Church
374 Zhongshan Middle Road
Quanzhou City

Xinjie Tang (New Street Church)
29 Taiguang Street
Xiamen (Amoy)
(Said by some sources to be the first Protestant Church in China)

Zhushu Tang (Bamboo Tree Church)
129 Kaihe Road
Xiamen

GANSU PROVINCE

This elongated province stretches just under 1,000 miles north and south and links old Turkestan (modern day Xinjiang) with Han China. Its capital, Lanzhou, which means "fragrant city", long served as a vital oasis on the old Silk Road which reached from the Chinese Empire to the Roman Empire and other European and Middle Eastern lands. The upper reaches of the Yellow River flows through central Gansu. Hundreds of miles of the Great Wall were built here during the Han Dynasty. In the south, winter wheat is the main crop. Stock breeding of cattle, sheep, camels and horses is common in the mountain and plains regions.

In the 1940s, Baptists of Jiangsu Province and Shanghai sent their own Chinese missionaries to begin churches in Gansu Province. Nurse Ruby Wheat, formerly of Yangzhou's Baptist Hospital, worked in the town of Wuwei in central Gansu until the 1949 liberation, when she transferred to medical work in South Korea. A leader in the Wuwei Baptist ministry was medical doctor Abraham Hsu. The Wuwei Church has been reopened. The Gansu Christian Council is at number 80 Zhangye Lu in Lanzhou.

Selected Gansu area church addresses:

Lanzhou Church
84, Zhangye Road
Lanzhou City

Xigu Church
Lanzhou City

GUANGDONG PROVINCE

This southernmost province is world renowned for its food. The majority of the overseas Chinese came from Guangdong province. The Chinese have a saying: "It is best to be born in Suzhou, marry in Hangzhou, eat in Guangzhou, and die in Lanzhou." The climate is best in Suzhou. The women are prettiest in Hangzhou. The food is finest in Guangzhou (capital of Guangdong and known in the West as Canton). The casket wood is superior in Lanzhou.

Guangzhou is about 90 miles northwest of Hong Kong and is 1,200 miles south of Beijing. It has developed many revolutionaries--men such as the Taiping Revolution emperor, Hong Xiuquan, and the founder of the Republic of China, Dr. Sun Yatsen (Sun Zhongshan).

Guangzhou was the first mission station of the American Southern Baptist Convention Foreign Mission Board. Baptist trivia: In 1846, I.J. Roberts, an independent Baptist missionary from Mississippi working loosely with the Boston Board in Guangzhou and Macau, was accepted via the mails as a Southern Baptist missionary. Baptist trivia: He was the first Southern Baptist missionary actually on foreign soil. Shuck returned with others as SBC missionaries.

Roberts was difficult to work with and resigned less than six years later. He remained in China, even spending a year with Hong Xiuquan in Nanjing's Taiping Heavenly Kingdom palace before leaving in 1866. His wife and two children had long before left him for the United States. Dale Carnegie's courses were too late for Roberts.

With the coming of R.H. Graves to Guangzhou in 1861, stability began to be in evidence. Graves remained active in China for 56 years.

The Zhanjiang oil harbor is a major research center for oil exploration and production. The church in this port city met for years in a home. In 1984 it moved into a reclaimed church building.

Southern Baptist missions were in central and western Guangzhou and Northern Baptist (now American Baptist Church) were in the eastern sections among the Chaozhou speaking peoples of Swatow (Shantou). Several outstanding Christian musicians are from Swatow, serving both in China and Hong Kong.

Selected Guangdong area church addresses:

Dongshan Church and
The Guangdong Union Theological Seminary
Dongshan District, 9 Sibei Tongjin
Guangzhou

Church of the Savior
184 Wan Fu Road, Guangzhou
(Built in 1903. Made the Cathedral of South China in 1953)

Meizhou City Church
Meixian

Shiqi Church
Gao Jia Ji, Taiping Road
Zhongshan City
(Sun Yatsen, Father of the Chinese Republic and a Christian, hails from Zhongshan area, just across the border from Macau.)

Shenzhen Church
Shenzhen (Across the river from Hongkong)
Shixi Church
146 Minquan Road
Shantou (Swatow City)

GUANGXI ZHUANGZU AUTONOMOUS REGION

This area, formerly called Guangxi province, came under Han Chinese rule later than some sections of China. The population has a majority of tribal peoples (the Zhuang, Dong, Yao, Miao, and the Yi minorities). There are churches among these people, as well as among the Han Chinese in the cities.

The area around Guilin is nothing less than a living, breathing example of Chinese scenic art. The mountains and hilly peaks are just as artists have pictured them for thousands of years. Han Yu, a Tang Dynasty poet, saw the rivers as a flowing green silk belt and the mountains as blue jade hairpins. Underneath the area are subterranean caverns and caves that match any in the world.

The church building in Guilin was built by Southern Baptists. It is on the main street and within easy walking distance of most hotels.

Southern Baptists had a thriving hospital in the river city of Wuzhou that is still thriving--now a city hospital without Christian connections. Dr. Bill Wallace served in the Stout Memorial Baptist Hospital until his death in 1951. Others who served in Guangxi that Jody and I worked with are retired. Among them: Mary and Oz Quick, Eloise and Baker J. Cauthen, Nan and Alex Herring and Millie Lovegren.

Southern Baptist Cooperative Services International educators Lou Ann and Kenneth Locke began teaching in Guangxi University, Nanning, in 1988. They taught at Yan'tai University before that. Ended up their foreign ministries in Russia.

Cooperative Baptist Fellowship continues to have a ministry at the Guangxi University under the capable leadership of Ina and Ron Winstead.

185

Selected Guangxi area church addresses:
Guilin Church [Former Baptist Church]
185 Zhongshan Zhong Lu
Guilin City

Nanning Church
65 Zhongshan Road
Nanning City

Wuzhou Church
5 Dazhong Road
Wuzhou City

Liuzhou Church
65 Deque Lu
Liuzhou City

GUIZHOU PROVINCE

The Chinese have a saying about this misty-mountainous province: "Never three days of clear bright weather, and nowhere three feet of flat land." The average altitude of the mountains is 3,200 feet. Populated mostly by the Miao, Buyi, Yi and Dong minority races, the province is rich in mineral resources. Coal fields, phosphorous deposits, copper, silver, and manganese are all abundantly mined.

Only 12 per cent of the land area is under cultivation -- with rice in the south and maize in the northwest. Guiding tobacco is popular throughout the country.

Guiyang is the capital. In modern times Zun Yi, located 120 miles north of Guiyang, has a bit of recent history. It was at Zun Yi, while on the Long March, that Mao Zedong took over leadership of the Communist Party Central Committee in January 1935.

One of the best books to come out of the Cultural Revolution came from a Guizhou native. Ms. Yue Daiyun, professor at Beijing University, shared her life with Carolyn

Wakeman who wrote her story in "To The Storm, The Odyssey of a Revolutionary Chinese Woman" (University of California Press: 1985).

Selected Guizhou area church addresses:

Guiyang Church
68 Qianning Xi Road
Guiyang City

Gebu Church
Hezhang County

HAINAN PROVINCE

In March of 1988 the island of Hainan was proclaimed a province of China. This 34,189 square kilometer island just off the coast of South China, mid-way between Hongkong and Vietnam, has a population of six million. Before becoming a province Hainan was part of Guangdong province.

In an attempt to bring the island into the twentieth century new land management regulations have been adopted. The island's authorities have the full power to manage and develop land on the island with local or foreign investors.

With modern management methods the island could become another Hawaii. Situated in the tropics it is ideal as a winter resort area. The chief cash crops are rubber, sugar cane, pepper, coffee, cashew nuts and soon Del Monte pineapples.

It was from this island that the famous Soong (Song) family got its start. Charlie Soong (a name he picked up on the way. He was born Han Chao-shun) stowed away on a 19th century ship to America from Hainan. He returned to China a Methodist missionary in the Shanghai area. He made his millions in publishing and other activities. His three daughters are easily the most famous Chinese sisters in China history. Soong Chingling (Song Qingling) married Dr. Sun Yatsen; Soong Ailing married Guomindang (KMT) Finance Minister H. H. Kung; Soong Meiling married Chiang Kai-shek (Jiang Jieshi).

Presbyterians led the way in early missionary work on the island.

Selected Hainan island church addresses:

Haikou City Church
Haikou

Yanyuan Village Church
Qiongzhong County
(Primarily Li and Miao Tribal Minorities people.
There are 10 churches in the county and five Meeting Points.)

Qiongzhong Church
Jiayi (Plus 7 Meeting Points, one in a hospital.

Qiongzhong Church
Qiongzhong City

HEBEI PROVINCE

Hebei means "north of the river" in Chinese, and it is a perfect name for this ancient province that lies mostly north of the Yellow River. Two of China's three municipalities, Beijing and Tianjin, are within Hebei's boundaries but not subject to the province. The Great Wall winds through the northern sections, and the Grand Canal begins at Tianjin and goes all the way south to Hangzhou. Shijiazhuang, four hours by train from Beijing, is the capital.

Springtime can be dusty, as winds transplant a lot of the Mongolian desert over this vast tableland. Iron and coal mines were badly hit by the July 28, 1976, earthquake that almost leveled the city of Tangshan and killed more than 700,000 people. On the tenth anniversary of the earthquake the city appeared to be completely re-built. A few damaged structures were left as a reminder of the tragedy. Wheat and cotton continue as the primary crops.

Selected Hebei area church addresses:

Shijiazhuang Church
#1 Shi Yi Lu
Shijiazhuang City

Baoding Church
Baoding City

HEILONGJIANG PROVINCE

This province's name means "Black Dragon River." It is named after the river of the same name that marks China's northernmost boundary with the Soviet Union. The shape of the province looks like that of a huge goose taking flight. The capital, Harbin, for many years just a small fishing village on the Songhua River, is in the middle of China's greatest wheat and corn producing areas. The city has a distinctly Russian atmosphere due in large part to the great numbers of White Russian refugees that fled there in 1917.

Once the largest Russian settlement outside the Soviet Union there are now very few Russians living in Harbin. The city's Ice Lantern Festival held in January and February is now the greatest tourist attraction. Ice sculptures of animals, buildings, bridges and legendary characters dominate the city.

In 1920 the Baptist churches of Shandong province sent their own Chinese missionaries to Harbin in Manchuria, now called Dongbei (The Northeast). Four years later the Chinese pastor in Harbin was joined by SBC missionaries Evelyn and Charles Leonard and Eula and C.E. James.

The Japanese invaded the area in 1931 and set up a puppet government in what they called Manchukuo. They made the last Qing emperor their puppet emperor over the area.

The Harbin Church was reopened December 23, 1980. Pastor Sun Yaozhong is senior pastor. Pastor Gu Shaotang was baptized in 1928 by Alfred Hansen, the father of Jorgen Hansen a Lutheran missionary from Denmark who was in language school with us in Taipei in 1957.

This particular church was built by German Lutherans. There are four new workers just graduated from the Dongbei Seminary in Shenyang: Miss Li Meilan who leads the Korean services that meet in the Harbin church building; Mr. Lu Dezhi, a young preacher; Miss Jin Huijie, who has just completed advanced study in religion at Beijing University; Deng Xixia, an evangelist.

Wang Muguang helps as much as he can at age 76. He is a 1940 graduate of the Huabei Baptist Seminary in Huangxian in Shandong province. He was a student there when C.L. Culpepper, Sr. was president of the school. Harbin is his home and he knows the Baptist history of the area.

Heilongjiang province has more than 600 home gathering places and 29 reopened or newly built churches. Churches have been opened in Qiqihar, Mudanjiang, Jiamusi, Yichun, Hegang, Jixi, Qitaihe and many other places. It is estimated there are 120,000 believers in the province.

The second church in Harbin was opened in the summer of 1987. It is in the former Baptist church that was built in 1936. The cornerstone is next to the gate and quotes Ephesians 2:20 that Christ is the cornerstone of the church.

Selected Heilungjiang area church addresses

Harbin Church
50 Dong Da Zhi Jie
Harbin (Built for Germans across the street from the Russian Eastern Orthodox Church in 1915.)

Beida Liudao Jie Church (6th Street Church)
222 Beida Liudao Jie
Harbin. (former Baptist Church)

Mudanjiang Church
Linkou County

Qiqihar Church
Qiqihar City

Eastern Orthodox Church
52 Dong Da Zhi Jie
Harbin

Formerly only Russians attend this church that was reopened
in 1981. At the time there were said to be only forty Russians
left in Harbin where there once were tens of thousands. Father
Zhu Shipu, the priest in charge, told me that to his knowledge
Harbin has the only active Eastern Orthodox Church left in
China.

One Eastern Orthodox (Dong Jing) Church is functioning
after a fashion in the city of Urumqi (Wulumuqi). According to
the Xinhua News Agency on May 10, 1983 150 Chinese citizens
of the Russian Nationality celebrated the traditional orthodox
Easter in Urumqi.

One Eastern Orthodox Church building in Shanghai, onion-
shaped domes and all, is located between the Jin Jiang Hotel and
the Hilton Hotel, just north of Huai Hai Middle Road. It is being
prepared for use as a museum. The frescoed domes though
damaged are still beautiful.

Russians form one of the smallest 50-plus Nationalities in
China. According to a census conducted in 1982 there were
2,662 Russians living in the Xinjiang Uyger autonomous region.

HENAN PROVINCE

The Yellow River runs through the northern reaches of this
province--hence its name, Henan, which means "south of the
river." No river has ever terrorized people the way the Yellow
River has. It is sometimes called "China's Sorrow." Henan's
capital for centuries was Kaifeng, a city that served also as the
capital for the Wei Dynasty (220-265 A.D.), and for the Liang,
Tang, Jin, Zhou and Northern Song dynasties. In the 1950s,
Zhengzhou became the capital of the province.

191

To walk along the foundations of city walls built before the time of Israel's King David is a historian's dream. To handle objects that were made before the monarchy was established in Israel is something I never thought I would do. Yet, here in this cradle of civilization, all this is still possible. The Shang Dynasty (2100 to 1400 B.C.) was located on the site of present-day Zhengzhou.

As the 20th century dawned, Southern Baptist missionaries working in Shandong and Jiangsu provinces began to investigate the possibility of opening work in Henan province. The David Herrings, Eugene Sallee and the W.W. Lawtons were among the first to open work in Kaifeng and Zhengzhou. The Huamei Baptist Hospital was begun by a Chinese doctor and then carried on by the Baptist missionaries. It is still ministering to the city of Zhengzhou and now is called the Number Three Hospital.

The hospital sits next to the sturdy Baptist church building that is now used by a clothing manufacturer. In May of 1984, a group of us walked through the old church with the late Maude Fielder (Mrs. Wilson Fielder, Southern Baptist missionary to Henan from 1914-1949). It could be reopened as a church if the manufacturer could locate other facilities for his operation. Zhengzhou has two newly built churches but more buildings are needed. I pray this old edifice may once again be used for the purpose for which it was built.

In our early years in the province of Taiwan, we had the once in a lifetime experience of working with many of the Henan missionaries. All are now retired and some have gone to be with the Lord. All had a special place in our hearts as they shared with us and the churches of Taiwan their love of China--and especially their love for Henan Province. Olive Lawton (born in Jiangsu province at the very time her father and Sallee were seeking to enter Henan), her brothers, W.W. Lawton, Jr., Deaver Lawton, and Alex Herring (son of David W. Herring who came to China in 1885) were born in China. They finished their missionary careers in Taiwan as my wife and I began ours.

Others who worked in Henan were Josephine Ward, Ola Lea, Addie Cox, the A. S. Gillespies, H. M. Harrises, G. W. Strothers, and the Buford Nichols, who opened Southern Baptist work in Indonesia. Many of these knew the importance of the churches of China being Chinese.

The first time I visited the Zhengzhou open church, in 1983, an 80-year-old pastor named Li asked me if I knew Rei Jiaoshi. He was speaking of missionary Katie Murray, with whom we had worked in the Kaohsiung (Gaoxiong) area of southern Taiwan. She had been Pastor Li's co-worker for nearly 20 years. He had not heard that she had died. I was grateful for the opportunity to know Katie better through Pastor Li.

Henan Province has churches in all the major cities and many Meeting Points all over country-side. Some rural areas have the most indigenous simple New Testament churches in the world. The most conservative estimates put the number of Christians in Henan at over one million.

Wu Huimin, a retired middle school teacher, and active member of the Zhengzhou Church shared with me his desire to record as much of the Christian history of Henan Province as he could in his remaining years. Pastor Wang Shengcai, outstanding woman pastor in Zhengzhou, told of the burden the people there have for training the laity. They have short-term Bible studies and church training courses in the church. The believers from the countryside come to the city for these times of refreshment and growth.

Kaifeng was a center of Jewish life in China about a thousand years ago. The Hebrew synagogue in Kaifeng was larger than any present-day synagogue. There is no trace of their heritage left in Kaifeng. In the 14th and 15th centuries they may have numbered as many as one thousand. In 1489 seventy families are recorded as being active in the worship of Jehovah. Details of the history of the Jewish community are recorded on three steles, dated 1489, 1512 and 1619.

Selected Henan area church addresses:

Zhengzhou Church
23 Hanchun Street
Zhengzhou

193

Kaifeng Church
24 Freedom Road
Kaifeng

Nanguan Church (Hospital Street Church)
South Suburb
Kaifeng

Hengyang Church
Zhongshan South Road
Hengyang City

Luoyang Church
49, Mingxin Street
Luoyang

Dong Fang County Church
Dong Fang Township
(Near the famous Shao Lin Temple Southwest of Zhengzhou.)

Xiaodian Church
Ruyang County, Luoyang

HUBEI PROVINCE

Hubei, which means "north of the lake," is almost the exact geographic center of Han China, being almost equidistant from Beijing in the north, Guangzhou in the south, Shanghai in the east and Chongqing in the west. Many of China's most famous fairy tales come from the Dongting Lake region that borders Hubei Province in Hunan Province.

The capital city of Wuhan is made up of three cities on the Yangzi River: Hankou, Hanyang and Wuchang. On October 10, 1911, the opening volleys of the revolution that finally overthrew the Qing Dynasty were sounded in Wuchang.

The great Yangzi River flows through the heart of these cities. This area is almost the center of Han China hence it is a crossroad of routes to all quarters of the land. The railway from Guangzhou to Beijing run north and south through the city. Ocean going ships traverse east and west on the mighty Yangzi.

Selected Hubei area church addresses:

Rongguang Tang (Glorious Light Church)
26 Huangshi Road (Yellow Stone Street)
Wuhan City

Wuchang Church and the
Zhong Nan (South-Central) Theological Seminary
187 Min Zhu Road
Wuchang-Wuhan

HUNAN PROVINCE

Hunan, meaning "south of the lake," is one of the leading grain producing areas. After rice, they grow a lot of maize, wheat, sweet potatoes, soya-beans, cotton, peanuts, tobacco and sugar cane. Cedar forests cover much of the mountains. Marco Polo spoke of the thick woods in the western plains of Hunan. The capital city, Changsha, was one of the last cities in China to hold out against the entrance of the foreign merchants and missionaries.

The most accessible coal fields of all South China are to be found in this province, a province that was early settled by Han peoples of the north. The valley corridors that the Hakkas (Kejia or Guest People) traveled as they migrated south to Guangdong, Taiwan, Hawaii and the world is a natural rail link for the north and south.

Hunan's most famous son was Mao Zedong. He was born on December 26, 1893, in the village of Shaoshan, 80 or so miles south of the capital of Changsha.

Hunan people like spicy hot food. Like their neighbors in Sichuan Province, they grow and eat a lot of chili peppers.

Selected Hunan area church addresses:

Changsha Church
115 Fan Xi Xiang,
Changsha City

Zhongshan South Road
57 Wai Xiang Chun Street
Changsha City

JIANGSU PROVINCE

Two tremendous rivers, the Huai and the Changjiang (better known as the Yangzi or Yangtze River), have helped make Jiangsu a fertile and productive province. The provincial capital Nanjing (former English spelling, Nanking), means "southern capital", and has served as the capital for many dynasties. For a time it also served as the headquarters for Chiang Kai-shek's Nationalist government. Nanjing was also the capital for the Taiping Heavenly Kingdom that dominated China's history from 1851 to 1864.

The beautiful city of gardens, Suzhou, was observed as a noble and grand city by Marco Polo in 1276. Located on the Grand Canal, it formerly was known as the Venice of China.

Southern Baptists built a hospital in Yangzhou, as well as schools and churches. In my hometown of Brownwood, Texas I visited with Dr. Ethel Pierce, whose parents went out in the 19th century as missionaries to China. She told of her own early experiences as a doctor in Yangzhou. I never thought I would see the day when I would visit her church in Yangzhou. But my wife Jody and I did just that in July of 1985. The old Baptist church was being renovated and used once again to the glory of God. It was a thrill to meet Pastor Wu Jishao, a Baptist from the old days, still carrying on for his Lord.

Very few pastors in China ever get to retire. Pastor Wu's brother, Wu Jizhong, was a Baptist leader in East China until his death in Shanghai in 1982. It was a treat to have Sunday evening dinner in the small one room apartment of Hua Puzhen

(Wu Jizhong's widow) and daughter Wu Yingguang as they graciously welcomed former co-worker and Southern Baptist foreign missionary Eloise Glass Cauthen to Shanghai.

In St. Paul's Church of Nanjing it was interesting to note that a baptismal pool had been added to this former Anglican Church. It is for any new converts that might prefer immersion to sprinkling as their mode of baptism. Stressing again the mutual respect Christians in China have toward the differing traditions and customs of other Christians.

One of China's greatest leaders came from northern Jiangsu province. Zhou Enlai was born in the ancient Grand Canal city of Huai An on March 5, 1898.

Selected Jiangsu area church addresses:

Mo Chou Road Church
390, Mo Chou Road
Nanjing

Saint Paul's Church
365, Taiping Road
Nanjing

Shan Xi Road Church
Nanjing,

Dachang Church
North of the Yangzi River from Nanjing
(The church met in a house and was featured in the 1985 Southern Baptist Foreign Mission Board film "Winter Is Past." They now have a new church building.)

Shitu Tang (former Methodist)
130 Yangyu Lane
Suzhou

Wuxi Church
96, Zhongshan Road
Wuxi

Yangzhou Church (Former Baptist Church)
Cuiyuan Road
Yangzhou

Zhenjiang Church
Da Xi Road
Zhengjiang

Huai Yin Church
65 Heping Road
Huai Yin City (Birthplace of Ruth Bell Graham, wife of evangelist Billy Graham.)

Nantong Church
Nantong City

Peixian Chahe Meeting Points
Xuzhou

Tongshan Church (Formerly Baptist)
Xuzhou (Visited by David Y. K. Wong, the first Chinese president of the Baptist World Alliance, 1979.)

JIANGXI PROVINCE

Though Jiangxi is land-locked, it has China's largest lake -- the 3,160-square-mile Lake Poyang. Some seventy percent of the farm land is used to grow rice in the province. Jiangxi's Nanfeng oranges are considered a treat all over China. The world's most famous porcelain comes from the little town of Jingdezhen, and Lu Shan is the favorite vacation spot of many Chinese leaders.

A turning point in the Chiang-Communist revolutionary struggle came in Nanchang on August 1, 1927. Zhou Enlai and

Zhu De defeated the Nationalist armies, and this event marked the birth of the People's Liberation Army. In China today, August 1 is officially Army Day.

In 1934 Chiang Kaishek began the New Life movement here. Chiang's son, Chiang Ching-Kuo was a special administrator in the southern city of Ganzhou.

The Long March that took Mao Zedong and his men on a dramatic two year (1934-35) escape from Chiang began in this province.

Unfortunately in some areas of China there are local Christian leaders more intent on being the boss than being the much needed shepherd and spiritual leader. In any organization there are those bad apples. The Three-Self Movement has persons in authority in some places who are more conscious of pleasing man than God. These men and women give the Movement a bad name. Some such people have seemed to surface more since the June 4, 1989, Tiananmen incident. The hardliners are coming out of the woodwork again like in the Cultural Revolution.

Selected Jiangxi area church addresses:

Nanchang Church
26-1, Changzheng Road
Nanchang City

Jiujiang Church
18, Dufu Lane
Jiujiang City

Lushan Church
20 Rizhao Feng
Lushan

Jingdezhen Church
292 Zhonghua Road
Jingdenzhen

JILIN PROVINCE

Formerly this area, along with Heilongjiang and Liaoning provinces, made up what was called Manchuria. The Russians ruled some areas, and the Japanese controled the area from 1933-1945.

When the city belonged to Japan, the last emperor of China lived here as a puppet ruler of Manchukuo, the name the Japanese called their colony. Emperor Puyi's palace is now the Jilin Provincial Museum.

Today, Changchun (Eternal Spring) is the capital of Jilin province. It was once known as the automobile manufacturing capital of the nation. The Changchun No. One Automobile Factory is one of China's largest automobile radiator making plants. Diesel engines especially for marine use are designed and built here. The latest in passenger trains are produced in Changchun.

Unique for China is a hospital named after a Canadian. The Bethune Medical University is named in honor of Dr. Norman Bethune for his service to the revolution. The school enrolls about 820 new students each year.

Most provinces have film and television production units and Changchun's film center is one of the best in the country.

The best apples and pears come from this area. Before the Cultural Revolution, the city had eight churches from seven different denominations.

In the whole province eight churches have been reopened, and there are an additional 40 home gatherings.

Koreans have their own autonomous region in Jilin called the Yanbian Korean Prefecture. A prefecture is smaller than a province but larger than a county (*xian*). This Korean prefecture covers some 41,500 kilometers.

When we visited Yanbian Korean Prefecture the capital Yanji was having its best weather before heading into a long cold winter. The Korean language was on every building, store and street sign. Many streets are paved but the walking areas are dusty and the area is poor when compared to East China.

East of Yanji is the town of Tumen where on Sunday October 18, 1987 Jody and I worshipped and rejoiced with the Korean Christians at a special service ordaining five new elders.

In the southeast corner of this prefecture is a mountain most sacred to all Koreans. Baitou Mountain is topped off with a gloriously blue lake in an ancient crater. The lake's name is most fitting: Lake of Heaven.

Two rivers divide China from Korea and they both have their source in the Changbai mountain range and forest preserve. Flowing east out of these mountains is the Tumen River and flowing west is the Yalu River.

Selected Jilin area church addresses:

Changchun Church
37 Xi Wu Ma Lu
Changchun City

Jilin Church
188 Henan Street
Jinlin City

Yanji Korean Church
28 Guangming Street
Yanji City

LIAONING PROVINCE

Liaoning borders on Korea and has a large population of Korean people. The capital city of Shenyang is shown on old maps as Mukden. It is the largest industrial city in northeastern China, majoring in electrical equipment, mining equipment and chemicals.

Every city in the province has at least one church open today. In addition, there are more than 50 home assembly gatherings. Ms. Wu Aien, a Korean lady pastor of the Xita Church in Shenyang, told me: "We have eight Korean churches and 18 meeting points in Liaoning province as of the summer of

1985." Close to two million Koreans live in the three provinces of Dongbei (northeast China: Liaoning, Heilongjiang, and Jilin).

In 1982 10,000 Korean Bibles were printed. A Korean language hymnal was published and another is in preparation. Pastor Wu Aien said the Koreans had merged their churches before the Japanese left China in 1945 and, thus, had a head start on the other China churches as they moved into the post-denominational era.

Shi Enfu, a 1987 graduate of the Dongbei Theological Seminary in Shenyang, told me there were at least ten Korean-language churches in Liaoning province. Shi has a heart for people, Chinese or Korean. Shi Enfu is now doing graduate study at Jinling Seminary in Nanjing.

Shi Enfu's family name *Shi* means "stone," His given name *Enfu* is made up of two Chinese words, *en* meaning "grace," and *fu* meaning "blessings" or "favor." In Chinese this word *fu* is also used to translate the word "Gospel."

Shi is a fifth-generation Christian and his depth of love for His Lord and desire to serve shows the great advantage of growing up in a Christian home.

Shenyang is the home of the Dongbei Theological Seminary (formerly called the Shenyang Seminary). When the church reopened in Shenyang, it was hard for Sun Jiaji to believe, because all his life that building had been a shoe factory. He went, he heard the gospel and soon was a believer and after God called him to preach, he entered seminary.

In nearby Fushun Wang Xiaoyin became interested in the Christianity from reading the many books his parents had. Though they were not Christians he soon became one, and also entered seminary in answer to God's clear call to him.

In the Korean border city of Dandong we met Miss Yao Rouman who works in the Yuanbaoshan Church. After her study in the Dongbei Seminary she returned to help Pastor Hou Baohua and deacon Wang Suiting.

In the Dongguan Church of Shenyang there is a woman pastor that leads her people with a love and devotion that is evident the first time you talk with her.She shares the pulpit and ministry with men pastors and church workers as equally as any

I have seen. She is Lu Zhibin and the 100-year-old former Presbyterian church has over 1000 in attendance every Sunday.

Another woman church worker working with Pastor Lu is Wang Yumin. She is the daughter of Wang Yangsan of Huangxian Baptist Seminary days. Pastor Wang and Qi Qingcai of Shanghai were like brothers as they grew up in the Baptist schools of Shangdong province in the 1920s.

Southern Baptist interest in Liaoning province began with visits by Matthew Yates of Shanghai in the 1860s. By the end of the 19th century Shandong believers were crossing the Bohai to Dalian sharing their faith. The Manchurian Baptist Mission began in 1925, five years after Shandong Baptists began sending their own missionaries to the area. They had a church in the port city of Dalian, and another in Harbin. The area is no longer called Manchuria. The Chinese call these three northernmost provinces *Dongbei*, which in English means Northeast.

Selected Liaoning area church addresses:

An Shan Church
Tie Dong District, An Shan City

Dongguan Tang (East Gate Church)
6, San Zhi Li,
Dadong Road, Section I

Xita Tang (West Pagoda Church, Korean)
17, Shi Fu Da Road, Section 2
Shenyang City,   Tel: 435-129

An Shan Korean Church
Tie Xi District, An Shan

Qidao Korean Church
155 Ren Zhong Jie
Dandong City

Yu Guang Street Church
2 Yu Guang Street, Zhongshan Distict
Dalian (seats 600 people)

Fushun City Church
Zhongyang Road, Xifu District
Fushun

Ying Kou Church
1 Yan Shou Li, Xi Shi District
Ying Kou City

NEI MENGGU
(INNER MONGOLIA AUTONOMOUS REGION)

Inner Mongolia is the largest geographic area of China after Xinjiang and Tibet. This was the first autonomous region to be created by the Communist government. The primary occupation is stock breeding. The majority of the people are Mongolian and speak the Mongolian language. It is believed that the Huns came from western Mongolia. The most famous of all Mongols-- Genghis Khan--conquered China and his grandson, Khublai Khan, founded and began the Yuan dynasty in the 12th century. Hohhot is the capital today. It is just 260 miles northwest of Beijing.

The eastern forests in Inner Mongolia represent 17 percent of all forest land in China. The area is rich in coal, iron, salt and soda.   The Mongolian language differs from Chinese in both sound and script. Inner Mongolia continues to use the classical alphabet written vertically while their cousins to the north in Outer Mongolia use the Cyrillic alphabet. Outer Mongolia has begun in recent years to let a little nationalism show through attempts to revive the ancient traditional script their cousins in China use.

Selected Inner Mongolia church addresses:
Hohhot Church
42, Da Xi Jie, Yuchuan District

Hohhot
Donghe Qu Tang
22, Da Mi Dou Street
Baotou

NINGXIA HUIZU AUTONOMOUS REGION

This area, small by China standards, nestles in with Gansu province and Inner Mongolia at the beginning of China's far west. The population is about two million, and one third of these are of the Hui nationality, or of the Islamic faith. The Great Wall and the Yellow River go right past the present-day capital of Yinchuan. Because it sits on a well watered plain Ningxia produces large quantities of rice and wheat. Some of the irrigation canals date back 2000 years.

Like their neighbor province of Gansu, Ningxia has several Buddhist monasteries that date back to the 5th century A.D. Some 30 miles northwest of the city of Guyuan in the Xumi Shan (Xumi Mountains), the Yuan Guang Monastery remains a constant reminder of the early movement of Buddhism from India to China.

Christians are few in this area, but churches have been reopened and new ones built, while many continue to worship in Meeting Points.

Selected Ningxia area church addresses:

Yinchuan City Church
20, Beijie, Yu Huan Ge
Yinchuan City

Pingluo County Church
Shizuishan City Church

QINGHAI PROVINCE

It seems strange to have a land-locked 9,800-foot plateau named "Blue Sea," which is what Qinghai means. The name comes from the huge lake in the eastern part of the province near the capital of Xining. Xining is a little northwest of Lanzhou, the capital of Gansu province. Qinghai province is inhabited by Khazak, Mongol and Tibetan herdsmen and some areas have fertile and extensive forests. It contains a great variety of wild animals. Salt is so abundant it is sometimes used for paving roads and for building bridges.

Tibetan Buddhism is evident in the temples and monasteries scattered over the area. One of the most interesting spots is the Labuleng Si. This is one of the six great monasteries of the yellow sect of Buddhism. Labuleng Si was built on the site of the Mongol prince's palace beginning about 1708.

The Christian church in the capital city of Xining in eastern Qinghai has been opened for worship. Pastor Meng Zhaohan helped the church to be reopened at Easter, 1981. In 1984 the church was rebuilt making it even more useful.

The Xining City Church is at number 14 Jiaochang Street in the capital city.

SHAANXI PROVINCE

It was here in 221 B.C. that the man who is called the First Emperor of China, Qin Shi Huangdi, set about to unify China. The country was called Qin, and it is probably from Qin (Ch'in) that we get the English name "China."

The capital, Xi'an, has been the capital for eleven dynasties. At one time the city (then called, Chang'an, or "Eternal Peace") was the largest city in the world. A Neolithic site, just six miles from Xi'an, was discovered in 1953. Artifacts uncovered indicate that the prehistoric Chinese were a clever people. At least those living in Banpo Village (and in neighboring Henan Province) 6,000 years ago were quite ingenious. Their farm tools and apparent fishing methods were ahead of the times!

The First Emperor got the ball rolling to build the Great Wall and had workmen begin on his tomb at the very beginning of his reign. Sima Qian, the great historian, records that more than 700,000 peasants worked on the project. Thousands of life-size terracotta warriors and horses that stood guard for 2,000 years have in recent years been re-discovered. The actual opening of the Emperor's tomb itself has had to be delayed.

In the Shaanxi Museum, among the forest of inscribed stones or stele, none is more interesting to the Christian than the one erected in 781 A.D. by the *Jingjiao* (popularly known as Nestorian Christians) that tells of their history and of a Persian known as Alopen.

One of the Jingjiao's hymns, "The highest heavens with deep reverence adore," is included in the 1985 edition of China's New Hymnal.

Some 270 miles north of Xi'an is the town of Yan'an. The Communist army's Long March of 1934-35 ended here. Yan'an became the headquarters for the Communists throughout the rest of the war with Japan and what we in the west call World War II.

Selected Shaanxi church addresses:

Xi'an Church
1 Nanxin Street, Jixian Lane
Xi'an

Dong Guang Church
Dong Xin Hang (Eastern suburbs)
Xi'an

The Shaan Xi Shengjing Xuexiao (Bible College)
San Yuan County Church, Xi'an (Opened March, 1988)

SHANDONG PROVINCE

Shandong, means "East of the Mountains," and is best known as the birthplace of Confucius (551-479 B.C.). He was not born in a huge and unified China, but in the state of Lu in the present city of Qufu in south central Shandong. The second greatest Chinese philosopher, Mencius, was also born in Shandong in 372 B.C.

Of the five holy mountains in China, Tai Shan, some miles north of Confucius' birthplace, is thought by many to be the greatest. Tai Shan has come to stand for strength and power that only the gods could provide. Many Chinese proverbs speak of Tai Shan (*shan* means mountain in Chinese). For example: *Tai Shan Bei Dou*, which says, "Mount Tai and the Big Dipper are both high and looked up to.". A phrase in praise of worthy men. Another example: *Tai Shan Ya Luan*, "To use Mount Tai to crush an egg!" The meaning is similar to the western idea of "overkill." You don't need an elephant gun to kill a mouse.

When China discovers the game *Trivial Pursuit* a good question would be: Which province of China has the longest coastline? Answer: Shandong.

Wheat, sweet potatoes and maize make up the primary food crops. Cotton, peanuts and tobacco are the main cash crops. Today Shandong is the number one peanut producing area in China. The province is well-known for peaches, pears, apples and grapes.

Jinan, the capital, is just three miles from the Yellow River. Neolithic pottery (6,000 B.C.) and Shang Dynasty (1711-1066 B.C.) objects have been uncovered in the nearby area.

Shandong became one of Southern Baptists' most interesting mission fields in the latter part of the 19th century and into the 20th century. In May 1859, Sallie Little Holmes and her husband Landrum Holmes visited the province and later moved there. Soon thereafter they were joined by the J.B. Hartwells and T. P. Crawfords. Holmes was likely killed by bandits outside Yantai in October 1861. T.P. Crawfords, with eleven years' experience in Shanghai, moved to Dengzhou in Penglai County. In 1873, Lottie Moon began nearly 40 years of service, mostly in the Pingdu township some 100 miles northeast of Qingdao.

Li Shouting, longtime pastor of a number of Shandong Baptist churches, was born just north of the village of Shaling near Pingdu. During the first quarter of this century he was responsible for more baptisms than any Baptist leader in China. He and many like him were well-taught by the little missionary from Virginia known as Lottie Moon (1840-1912).

Dr. T.W. Ayers led in opening the first hospital with a continuing ministry that was related to Southern Baptist missions. This was 1903 in the town of Huangxian. A seminary was opened in the same area the following year. Dr. and Mrs. C.L. Culpepper, Sr., went to China in 1923 and worked nearly 20 years in Shandong. Our first eight years as missionaries to Taiwan were Ola and Charles Culpepper's last years on the field. We learned to love and appreciate Shandong and Shandong people from them.

The old Baptist church building in Yan'tai is now the Catholic Church there. When I worshipped there I could almost feel the spirit of men like W.B. Glass, Li Shouting and Wang Yangsan of by-gone Baptist days.

The late Bishop Stephen Wang (Wang Shenyin) of Jinan told me there are over 60 churches open in Shandong by 1985 and that there were another 2,000 home gatherings for believers. It is estimated that there are 250,000 Christians in the province. The churches early on sent 12 students to study at Jinling Seminary in Nanjing and 13 students to the Hua Dong Seminary in Shanghai before the Shandong Seminary opened.

The Penglai (formerly Deng Zhou) Church on Monument Street that Martha Foster and T. P. Crawford built and where Miss Lottie Moon worshiped was reopened for worship in 1988. The city has around 100 Christian households. The Monument Street Church building has a 1911 marble plaque in Chinese about Martha Foster Crawfords' work and a 1915 *beiji* (an upright stone stele or tablet that with inscribed words of record or praise.) telling of the work of Miss Lottie Moon. Bishop Stephen Wang agreed it would be a good idea to add another marble plaque telling of the work of the Chinese pastors of the Penglai Church.

Bishop Stephen Wang told me early on of his hope that Shandong one day could train church leaders for their area. His dream of a Shandong seminary became a reality in September 1987 when classes began in the city of Jinan. Bishop Wang was elected president by his Shandong peers.

Selected Shandong church addresses:

The Jinan Church
425, Jing 4 Street
Jinan City

Wei Yi Road Church
Nan Shang Shan Jie
Jinan City

Huangxian Town Church (Former Baptist compound)
Huangxian

Guangrao Meeting Point
Dongying City

Bei Ma Lu Church
Huangxian Town

Yantai Church
New World Street
Yan'tai City

Qingdao Church
15, Jiangsu Road
Qingdao

Si Fang Church
15 Jia He Road
Qingdao

Penglai Church (Formerly Baptist)
Monument Street, built about 1869.
Penglai

Pingdu Church

Pingdu County (Remnant of the Muen Baptist Church worshipping not far from the former Baptist hospital and a block from the Pingdu Hostel.)

SHANGHAI CITY

China's most densely populated city sits just south of the mouth of the Changjiang, the world's third greatest river after the Amazon and the Nile. Near Shanghai the river is called the Yangtze or Yangzi River. The city is just about on a latitude with Houston, Texas, but the climate is not the same. The climate can be as muggy as Houston's in the summer, but it is much colder in winter. The city covers an area of 2,355 square miles and has more than 12 million people.

This most western-appearing city of China is the center of trade and commerce. It is a trend-setter and, in recent years, has begun to regain much of the color and flash of former years. At the end of 1989 there were 23 Protestant churches buildings in use and hundreds of Meeting Points (sometimes called "house churches" overseas) serving this vast city. The city has been a center for Christian ministry for most of the past 140 years. Many foreign missionary groups began work here early, as did Southern Baptists with the coming of the J. Lewis Shuck and the Matthew T. Yates families in 1847. Both these men built homes just outside the wall of the old Chinese city, just west of the North Gate, near today's Renmin Road. The First Baptist Church (or Old North Gate Church) was organized November 6, 1847. Charter members along with the Yates and Shucks, Eliza and Thomas William Toby were two Chinese men named Yang and Mun, who came with the Shuck and Toby families from Canton. The present building is on the corner of Fujian and Renmin Road.

The present building of the First Baptist Church was built in 1920. The five-storied church was untouched by the Red Guards of the 1960s and has served as a primary school since 1958. In Southern Baptist mission history, it had the longest continuous existence of any Baptist Church in China -- 111 years.

The First Baptist Church of Shanghai is not among Shanghai's reopened churches. It, like many unopened churches, is used in other ways today. (Besides the fine primary school using much of the property in 1988, the worship center, long used by the school was made into a high class billiard parlor.) Saint Peter's Episcopal Church is another example. It is not reopened as a church, but is used by the hospital next door.

R.T. Bryan arrived in Shanghai in 1886. Bryan's first two years of mission work were Matthew T. Yates' last two. The Bryan's old red-brick home still stands. It is now the home for several families, including the home of the widow of Baptist pastor Shepherd Zhang.

The Huadong (East China) Seminary opened September 11, 1985. The late Bishop Sun Yanli was the first principal and the late Dr. Qi Qingcai ("Charlie Chi") the first chairman of the seminary board. After outgrowing the space at the Grace Church, the 1986 classes met in the Muen Church in downtown Shanghai. They began the second year with 80 students and held their first graduation service in 1989. In the summer of 1989 the Huadong Seminary moved to number 71 Wu Yuan Road. An expanded seminary campus with all new buildings in the the process of being built. You can view the proposed campus on the Internet. Go to the Towery site called Mission Forum <www.laotao.org/mission/> and then to seminaries.

Selected Shanghai area church addresses:

Guoji Libaitang
53 Heng Shan Road
Shi Qigui, senior pastor.

Huai En (Grace Church)
375 Shaan Xi Bei Road

Muen Church
316 Xizang Middle Road

Qing Xin Church (Pure Heart Church)

30 Da Chang Street

Hu Xi Church (West Shanghai Church)
1456 Chang Ning Road

Jingling Church
135 Kun Shan Road
425 Fu Xing Road

China Christian Council
Three-Self Committee offices
Tian Feng Monthly Magazine
169 Yuanmingyuan Road
Shanghai

Interesting bit of trivia: The National and local Offices of the China Christian Council and the Three-Self Movement Committee are one block south of the former Baptist True Light Building, where the offices of the Southern Baptist Mission and China Baptist Convention were located. Built in the 1920s it also had a radio studio, a Christian bookstore and classrooms for the downtown business branch of Shanghai University, founded by American and Southern Baptists in 1905.

SHANXI PROVINCE

Shanxi means "west of the mountains," and in the Taiyuan Basin there are located some of the world's largest coal and iron deposits. A harsh climate makes the winters difficult because it is then that the strong winds from Mongolia blow in from the north. The Shanxi merchants rival those of Ningbo (Zhejiang Province) for their ability at banking and trading.

The Boxer Rebellion of 1900 was especially tragic here. Many missionaries and local Christians were killed. Taiyuan, a city of more than one million people, is the present capital of Shanxi province. From the fall of the Qing Dynasty in 1911 until the liberation of 1949, the northern warlord, Yan Xishan, ruled the city with an iron fist.

213

Timothy Richards, pioneer British Baptist missionary, was instrumental in the building of a Christian university in Taiyuan. Today that school is used as the provincial normal (teacher's) university. There are about a thousand Christians in Taiyuan, including those in numerous home gathering points.

Selected church addresses:

Taiyuan Church
98 and 118 Qiao Tou Jie
Taiyuan City

Datong City Church
Datong

Yaodian Church
Xianyang City

SICHUAN PROVINCE

The southwest China province of Sichuan, which means "Four Rivers," is famous for pandas (there are eight protected areas for them), hot peppers (especially *doufu* cooked in a spicy-hot mixture of meats and sauces), and people (there are more than 100 million of them in this single province).

The tremendously high and rugged mountains inspired the eighth century poet, Li Bai, to write: *Shu dao nan, nan yu shang qing tian.* In not-so-poetic English this translates: "Sichuan roads are more difficult to travel than the road to heaven."

The late Deng Xiaoping, the man most responsible for the ten years of progress in opening China to the modern world, 1979-89, is a native of Guang'an County in central Sichuan. He was born August 22, 1904 to the second wife of his Guangdong Hakka father, who was said to be a village official. Deng Xiaoping (not the name he was born with) comes from a very traditional Chinese family.

Chinese officials almost never give interviews so biographical information is difficult to obtain. For a good account of Deng's life read David Bonavia's *Deng,* published by Longman, Hongkong, 1989.

Some time in the year 250 B.C., many engineers put together an irrigation system that is still working. The Dujiang Yan Dam, some 25 miles northwest of Chengdu, the capital, has to be seen to be believed. During the early years of the project it made possible the irrigation of more than one million hectares of land. And today, after all these centuries it irrigates well over sixteen and a half million acres of farmland.

One of China's five sacred mountains is in the south-central part of Sichuan. Mount Emei stands 10,143 feet above sea level. To the Chinese, mountains are often likened to the firmness and constancy that all men strive for. The 1,200-year-old, 389-foot colossal Buddha sits near Mount Emei over looking the Min River.

Chongqing (Chungking), the city without bicycles, sits on hills in the south and is the main port for the Yangtze River boats that go all the way to Shanghai. Chongqing was the Nationalist Chinese headquarters toward the close of World War II.

American Baptist Church and later the Conservative Baptist Society missionaries worked this area, along with hosts of other denominations. My wife went with Millie Lovegren in the summer of 1984 to revisit the place of Millie's birth in Ya'nan (Yenan), just north of Mount Emei. Her parents were Baptist missionaries nearly 40 years ago in Sichuan. Her father, Lee Lovegren, was imprisoned in Ya'an by the communists in 1951. It was four long years before he was allowed to leave China. One thing I have always liked about Millie is that she was a "people person." Projects and programs are fine, but to Millie "people" were more important. I think it was something she got from her earthly mother and father and it was refined by her Heavenly Father. Read more on Mildred Lovegren in *Millie's China*, a book by her sister Edie Lambert.

Selected church addresses:

Shangxiang Street Church

Chengdu City

Chongqing Church
96 Ci Qi Street,
Chongqing

Nan'an Tang (South Bank Church)
Shang Xin Street
Chongqing

Leshan Church
9, Xing Fa Street
Leshan Township

TIANJIN CITY

This industrial giant of North China sits on a latitude close to that of Washington, D.C. in the United States. The city extends along the Hai River, two hours by train from Beijing. The city's most famous products are its carpets. There are eight factories producing an estimated 150,000 square yards of carpet every year. The population is more than seven million.

The city also is the home of one of my favorite eating places: the Goubuli Baozi restaurant. This name "Goubuli" is interesting. Literally it means "Even the dogs will not have it"! It was a nick-name given to the owner of this resturant when he was a small boy. When years later he went into the business of making and selling "baozi", steamed bread wrapped around minced meat and vegetables, he used his nick-name: Goubuli Baozi, "Baozi Even The Dogs Won't Eat"! The restaurant's steamed "baozi" are the best in the world. They are beautiful to look at, have a terrific aroma, and are wonderful to eat. The restaurant is a handy place, too. It is located on Shandong Street, just a block from the Christian church.

Tianjin (spelled Tientsin on old maps), along with Beijing and Shanghai is one of only three cities that are responsible directly to the central government in Beijing.

The city was besieged by the Taiping troops in 1853 and has been occupied by the English, French and Japanese at various times over the last one hundred years.

Tianjin University claims to be the oldest western-style university in China. Christian foreign missionaries began the school in 1895.

Selected Tianjin area church addresses:

Tianjin Church
237 Binjiang Road, Heping District,

Cangmenkou Church
Cangmenkou

Tianjin YMCA
12 Guangxi Road, Tel: 397-364

Tianjin YWCA
6 Changle Li
Chong Qin Dao, Tel: 318-498

XINJIANG UYGUR AUTONOMOUS REGION

This land of the Silk Road was, until the invention of the compass, the only known safe route of commerce between Europe and the lands of China. Along these roads Buddhism entered China. Along these roads Marco Polo entered China. As Chinese influence in the area waned, the Arab empires grew stronger. Hence, the Islamic faith is a major religious power in the region. In the city of Kashgar, the Id Kah Mosque -- said to be the largest in China -- can hold 8,000 worshippers. The non-Han people are the Uygurs, Kazakahs, Mongolians and many others--all speaking and looking like their forebearers from the Middle East and elsewhere.

Xinjiang is an area four times the size of France with more than 13 million people. In time, with proper planning, it could become the garden spot of the world. Urumqi (or Wulumuqi in

Chinese) is the capital of the region. It is almost 2,000 miles west of the nation's capital in Beijing. The region borders the former Soviet Union, Afghanistan, Pakistan, India, and Mongolia.

About 60 miles southeast of Urumqi is the city of Turpan in one of the world's lowest elevations. It is 505 feet below sea level. Stifling hot in summer, Turpan has cold dry winters. Hami melons are loved all over China.

The church in Urumqi reopened in 1980 and has about 1,000 members. It is estimated that there are about 15,000 Christians in the whole Xinjiang region. In July of 1984 the Urumqi Church ordained one elder and 14 deacons. Pastor Li Kaihuan began the Urumqi Church in 1954. Pastors Chen and Huang presently lead the congregation at the main church and for many of the Home Meeting Points in the area.

In southeast Xinjiang the Aksu (Akesu) Church is the largest church in the province. It seats 750 people and has about 2000 members. Brother Tang Yuanmo, age 58 and not yet ordained, leads this growing congregation. A nearby Bing Tuan (retired army villages) has regular services led by retired soldier Liu Shaolong.

Selected church addresses:

Urumqi Church
1, Ming De Road
Urumqi Aksu

Aksu Church
Jiankang Road

Shihezi Church
94 Lao jie
Shihezi City

XIZANG (Tibet Autonomous Region)

The mystique of Tibet remains as strong with me today as when, in high school, I read of trips made there by various explorers, journalists, and adventurers. The roof of the world! The red and white palace of Potala in Lhasa! Dalai Lamas! Yak butter! Miles and miles of grassland. Mountains that are eternally packed in ice and snow.

Yet Tibet is more than that -- it is people. A very few of them have ever heard of the resurrected Christ or of the faith of our fathers. Lamaism is a form of Mahayana Buddhism, with local color added wherever it goes. This form of Buddhism is not confined to Tibet. The Mongols have another variation, and the largest Lama temple outside of Tibet is located in Beijing.

Tibet was a theocratic state for centuries. Monks, priests and monasteries had the final say in any decision. Until 1950 when the Chinese People's Liberation Army marched in, it was a very primitive society. Most of the people were slaves of the landlords or of the monasteries. The people were kept under control by horrendous penalties such as eye-gouging and tongue-slitting.

A revolt broke out in Tibet in 1958. With their power slipping from them the monks began spreading the story that the Chinese had levied taxes on the images of the Buddha and were out to eliminate the monasteries. They would eliminate Buddhism in Tibet. This rallied the people to revolt against the Chinese. The most reliable reports were in the *London Times* and the *Daily Express* British newspapers in 1958-59.

The Dalai Lama, winner of the 1989 Nobel Peace Prize for his non-violent approach to helping his people, had already fled to India. Though the Dalai Lama has been gone from Tibet nearly 40 years the Tibetans still want him back. In Guangzhou I learned this first-hand. I met some Tibetans near the railway station. It was a rather cool January afternoon and they were dressed much warmer than the local Cantonese. They had on their normal winter furs. Since I do not speak Tibetan I asked one of them in Chinese if he was from Tibet. He answered in Chinese saying yes and asked where I was from. I told him and his next question was, "Have you seen our Dalai Lama? We need him, we want him to come home." He had no fear as he spoke this boldly. Such words could land the man in a lot of trouble in China today. But he said it again and again. It was all he wanted to talk about. His heart yearned for the only God he knew and he did not care who knew it.

According to the latest State Nationalities Commission statistics, there are 2.02 million ethnic Tibetans in Tibet (as against 1.2 million in 1959 and in all of China today there are 3,870,100). Tibet has 73,000 Han Chinese living there. There are also 7,000 Menbas, 2,000 of Hui, Luba and Naxi origin. During 1981-87 the Chinese government spent more than a million U.S. dollars a year just restoring temples alone. Much more has gone into schools and hospitals. Much of this good has been overshadowed by the government crackdown in March 1988 and the subsequent martial law, still in effect in 1990.

There are a few Christians in Tibet today. To my knowledge, there are Christian believers but no active Christian worship centers or churches in Tibet.

The northern section is one huge tableland over 16,000 feet up. So barren, cold and dry, that some travelers think it makes the Gobi Desert look fertile by comparison. The famous Himalaya mountains range across southern Tibet.

Lhasa, "the Forbidden City of the Lamas" sits on almost the same latitude as Houston Texas and Cairo Egypt but differs from these cities as it is 11,830 feet above sea level. The Potala palace is supposed to have been built in the seventh century. It was the living quarters for the Dalai Lamas and contained the library of Tibet's sacred books.

The city is amost circular in shape with narrow but straight streets. Chinese occupation of Lhasa in 1722 brought to an end the great walls that surrounded the city.

Lhasa has always been a city of pilgrimages. This makes for a plus in the economy as all kinds of retail trade prosper. Much of this retail trade is in the hands of the women.

Little reliable information comes out of Tibet today. Tibet would have a difficult time trying to survive as an independent country surrounded as she is by unfriendly neighbors. But with humane Chinese leadership and their god-king, the Dala Lama, to guide them living standards and the welfare of the people of Tibet could be made much better.

YUNNAN PROVINCE

On his journey through Yunnan (*land of the southern clouds*), Marco Polo reported that in Kunming, the capital, he saw "a few Christians...who are Nestorians." The Jingjiao believers mentioned earlier.

In modern history, the city of Kunming got a late start. It was only in 1832 that the walled city began to take on any prominence. It was a center of activity during the war with Japan and in World War II. The terminus for the famed Burma Road was Kunming. In those days it was the only way of getting supplies to the Nationalist Chinese and American forces in China.

The province borders Burma, Vietnam and Laos--where there are still some disagreements with the Vietnamese.

Some 60 miles southeast of Kunming is the famed petrified or Stone Forest. Some of these unusual rock formations rise abruptly to more than 100 feet in the air. The explorer will find his match here.

Selected church addresses:

San Yi Tang (Trinity Church)
218 Wucheng Road
Kunming

Holy Zion Church (Opened April 15, 1981)
61 Jin Bi Road
Kunming

Dali Church
Dali

Lan Chang Xian
Dai Minority Church
Dai Minority Church

Throughout Yunnan province the various non-Han nationalities have grown and are growing interesting indigenous churches. Along the border with Burma many from both countries often worship and work together with little thought of man-made boundaries and restrictions.

ZHEJIANG PROVINCE

This East China coastal province -- along with its neighbor to the north, Jiangsu -- is a prosperous industrial and agricultural center. Hangzhou, the capital, is just three and a half hours by train from Shanghai. It is built around one of China's best known scenic and vacation spots -- the West Lake. Everyone who visits Hangzhou will be told the old saying, "Above is heaven, and below is Hangzhou and Suzhou."

There are now more than one million Christians in Zhejiang. In this one province there are now more Christians than all China's Christian believers prior to 1949. There are now more than 1,000 church buildings -- many newly built in the country-side with more going up all the time. The churches in the villages I visited ate together and fellowshipped together in a manner that said: "This is the center of activity and the most important activity in this village!"

Zhejiang also has the only Christian Middle School in China today. It is the Yangzhen (*bring forth true knowledge*) Christian Middle School and was begun by the Longquan Christian Church in 1985. Longquan County is located 400 km south of Hangzhou. East of Longquan the port city of Wenzhou (said to be the button capital of the world) probably numbers more Christians per square foot than anywhere in China. Wen Zhou was a favorite among early Arab merchants.

Due east of Hangzhou is Ningbo. The Ningbo Church had the faith to open first after the Cultural Revolution. Ningbo is the old home place for Chiang Kaishek (Jiang Jieshi) and his son, Chiang Ching Kuo (Jiang Jingguo), the Nationalist leader in Taiwan.

Three of Ningbo's most noted native sons have been prominent in Hong Kong and world affairs: Sir Y.K. Pao (Bao

Yugang), possibly the world's richest shipping magnate at one time, and the 29th generation direct descendant of the famous Judge Bao Zhang, a Song Dynasty minister more popularly known as Bao Gong -- a name synonymous in China with justice. Another is Sir Run Run Shaw, film maker and philanthropist (the only one of the three I met personally). The third Ningbo man was Dr. T.K. Ann, business - man and author of books on the Chinese language.

In addition to these three men, another Ningbo native has been the deputy head of the Hong Kong office of the Xinhua New Agency, Mr. Li Chuwen. Mr. Li is a graduate of the old Baptist university (*Hujiang*) in Shanghai. He was for a time pastor of the Community Church of Shanghai. So it just may be true that Ningbo men were behind Shanghai's great days of the past and have meant a lot to Hong Kong's dynamic personality.

About half way between Hangzhou and Ningbo sits the town of Shaoxing. Lu Xun (1881-1936), father of modern Chinese fiction, was born in Shaoxing. Qiu Jin (1875-1907), a early revolutionary heroine, was also born here. The most famous industry is the celebrated Shaoxing yellow wine.

In former days missionaries often named hospitals, schools and even churches in memory of outstanding pioneer missionaries. Baptist had memorial schools named for Graves, Rankin, Yates and many more. Others did the same. Now it is fitting to see the name of a church in Hangzhou named in honor of that church's first Chinese pastor. It is the former Presbyterian Church, now the Si Cheng Church.

Selected church addresses:

Si Cheng Tang (Church)
104, Jiefang Road
Hangzhou

Drum Tower Church
24 Bu Shi Xiang
Hangzhou

Tian Shui Tang (Heavenly Water Church)
Zhongshan Bei Road
1, Yesu Xiang (Jesus Lane)
Hangzhou

Ningbo Church
Ningbo City
(The first church to reopen after the Cultural Revolution.)

Wenzhou City has four large churches and many meeting points.

Xixing Village Church
Shaoxing County
(South of Hangzhou. This church was one of several featured in the award-winning 1985 Southern Baptist Foreign Mission Board film, "Winter Is Past.")

OUTLINE CHRONOLOGY OF
CHINESE HISTORY
AND
SELECTED CONTEMPORARY WORLD EVENTS

I. Prehistory Dynasties:
- (1) **Xia Dynasty**, 21 to 16 centuries B.C.
  - -- 2000 B.C. The Bronze Age began
- (2) **Shang Dynasty**, 1766-1122 B.C.
  - -- China silk industry already famous
  - -- The time of the Judges; Moses and Joshua
  - -- David was king of Israel

II. Zhou (Chou) Dynasties:
- (1) **Western Zhou**, 11th century to 771 B.C.
  - -- 1193 B.C. The Greeks destroy Troy
  - -- King Solomon's Temple built (c. 1000 B.C.)
  - -- Judah-Israel Civil War
- (2) **Eastern Zhou**, 770-256 B.C.
  - -- Early years of Isaiah and Amos.
  - -- Time of Zoroaster and Buddha (563?-483?).
- (3) **Spring and Autumn Period**, 770-476 B.C.
  - -- The prophet Jeremiah's lifetime
  - -- 586 B.C. Solomon's Temple destroyed
  - -- 551-479 B.C. China's philosopher Confucius, a contemporary of Ezra
  - -- 516 B.C. Zerubbabel rebuilds the Jewish Temple at Jerusalem
- (4) **The Warring States**, 475-221 B.C.
  - -- Nehemiah rebuilds the walls of Jerusalem.
  - -- The book of Malachi, the end of the Old Testament
  - -- Philosopher Mencius born 372 B.C.
  - -- Philosopher Aristotle (384-322 B.C.)
  - -- Alexander the Great conquered "the known world" (356-323 B.C.)

III. Qin (Chin) Dynasty, 221-207 B.C.

-- 218 B.C. Hannibal crosses the Alps and invades Italy
-- China unified under the First Emperor who began the building of the Great Wall; buried scholars alive and burned their great books
-- The period between the Old and New Testaments
-- The Silk Road to Europe was already famous
-- China establishes medical schools, emphasis on preventive medicine

IV. Han Dynasty, 206 B.C. to A.D. 220

-- China unified in a much kinder fashion
-- 164 B.C. Judas Maccabeus rededicates the Temple at Jerusalem
-- The time of Christ.
-- 70 A.D. The Romans destroy the Jerusalem Temple
-- The Apostle John writes the book of Revelation on Isle of Patmos (c. 100).
-- The earliest known use of paper, called *Baqiao,* found in Baqiao, China.
-- 150 A.D. Justin Martyr wrote there were people *everywhere* that served and worshipped the crucified Jesus and Father of all mankind

V. The Period of the Three Kingdoms: Wei, Shu, Han and Wu, 220-280 A.D.

VI. The Western and Eastern Jin Dynasty, 221-420.

-- 411 A.D. Saint Augustine wrote *City of God*

VII. The Northern and Southern Dynasties:

(1) Southern Song, Qi, Liang and Chen, 420-589.

-- Attila (406?-453), King of the Huns.

228

(2) **Northern: Northern Wei, Eastern Wei, Northern Qi, Western Wei, and Northern Zhou**, 420-581.

-- 529, The Benedictine Order established

VIII. Sui Dynasty, 581-618.

-- 622 A.D. Mohammed fled to Medina
-- China, using woodblocks, begins the earliest form of printing.

IX. Tang Dynasty, 618-907.

-- China's golden age - Poets Li Bai and Du Fu
-- A physician, Sun Simiao, records the first recipe for gunpowder.
-- 635-845 The Nestorians (*Jingjiao*) introduce Christianity. These Syrian Christians not paid or sent by institutions or mission boards
-- 635 A.D. Syria conqured by Islam
-- 701 Codification of Japanese law
-- 794 Buddhism established in Kyoto, Japan

X. The Period of the Five Dynasties: The Later Liang, Later Tang, Later Jin, Later Han and Later Zhou, 907-960.

XI. Song Dynasty 960-1279.

-- Chinese culture abounds.
-- China invents the compass and begins the "blue and white" or *qinghua,* underglaze porcelain.
-- 1209 Francis of Assisi (1182-1226) begins the Franciscan Order
-- 1163 Jews build a temple in Kaifeng and rebuild it in 1279 (According to a 1489 stele inscription).

> -- Between 1163 and 1688 this synagogue restored at least ten times (According to Sidney Shapiro)

XII. Liao Dynasty 916-1125.
> -- 1000, Eric the Red discovers Greenland; his son Leif Erkson discovers America.
> -- 1066, The Normans invade England
> -- 1096 The First Crusade to oust Muslims from Palestine

XIII. Jin Dynasty 1115-1234.
> -- 1162-1227?, Genghis Khan unites the Monguls. His armies push as far as Poland. 1240 Monguls capture Moscow
> -- 1167 Oxford University founded in England
> -- The Magna Charta, the great charter of English political and civil liberties, granted by King John on June 15, 1215

XIV. Yuan Dynasty(Monguls) 1271-1368.
> -- 1261-1294 Kublai Khan, Genghis Khan's grandson, conquers China and founds the Yuan Dynasty.
> -- 1271 Marco Polo (1254?-1324?), at age 17, goes with his father and uncle to China.
> -- 1291 Crusades end as Muslims rout Christians in Palestine

XV. Ming Dynasty 1368-1644.
> -- John Huss (or Jan Hus) (1369?-1415), a Bohemian Christian reformer was burned at the stake.
> -- 1371-1435, China admiral Zheng He. He sails to Africa. Even after his great voyages Mings decide to close China forbidding travel and trade. The conservatives see no need of advancement beyond the status quo.

(Not the first nor last time such thinking controled the Chinese empire and peoples.)

-- 14th - 16th centuries, European Renaissance
-- The European Church Reformation: Martin Luther (1483-1546)
-- Francis Xavier (1506-1552).
-- In 1492 Columbus sailed the ocean blue.
-- The ships of Magellan (1480-1521) circle the globe.
-- With the baptism in Switzerland January 21, 1525 of George Blaurock by Conrad Grebel the Anabaptists denomination was born. They dared to form a church after the New Testament pattern, thus leaving behind both the Roman Catholic and Luther's Reformation patterns
-- 1534 The Jesuit order is founded by St. Ignatius Loyola
-- 1545 &1563 The Council of Trent
-- 1564-1616 William Shakespeare's times
-- 1565 The Jesuits begin work in Macau
-- 1588 The Spanish Armada defeated by English
-- 1610 Death of Jesuit Matteo Ricci in Peking
-- 1607 The Jamestown Colony begun in America
-- 1620 English Puritans found the Plymouth Colony
-- 1628-1688, John Bunyan, Baptist author of *Pilgrim's Progress*, spends years in jail for his faith

XVI. Qing (Ching) Dynasty, 1644-1911.

-- The Manchus from the northeast conquer China; overthrow of the Mings takes a generation
-- 1776, July 4, American Independence

231

- -- 1807 Robert Morrison, the first Protestant missionary to China arrives in Macau
- -- 1818-1883 Philosopher Karl Marx
- -- 1836 The beginning of Baptist missions to China in 1836
- -- 1836 The Republic of Texas is established
- -- 1839 & 1860 The Opium Wars
- -- 1843 Hong Kong is ceded by China to Britain
- -- 1845, May, the American Southern Baptist Convention organized in Atlanta, Georgia
- -- 1847, Nov., 6, The First Baptist Church of Shanghai (Old North Gate Church) founded by Matthew T. Yates and wife Liza
- -- 1851-1864 The Taiping Revolution
- -- 1899-1900 The Boxer Rebellion
- -- 1910 The Edinburgh Missionary Conference

XVII. The Republic of China, 1911-2000

- -- Since 1949 this Republic has governed only the province of Taiwan
- -- Sun Yatsen is considered the Father of the Republic of China; Taiwan and PRC issue stamps honoring him
- -- President Chiang Kai-shek and later his son led the Nationalists in Taiwan
- -- The present President, Li Teng Hui, became a dedicated Christian through the friendship of several Christians, including Southern Baptist's first Taiwanese-speaking missionary, Richard E. Morris (1928-85)
- -- Arizona becomes USA's 48th state in 1912
- -- China Communist Party organized, 1 July 1921
- -- Herman Liu Chan-En (1896-1938) first Chinese President of Baptist's Hujiang (Shanghai) University is assassinated by Japanesse. Made a national hero in the PRC

XVIII. The People's Republic of China, 1949-Present

-- A peace treaty between the two "republics" has never been signed, hence they coexist, each claiming to the be the rightful ruler of China

-- Mao Zedong led the communists to a mainland victory with the able help of Zhou Enlai, October 1, 1949.

-- China's Great Leap Forward (1958-1960)

-- China's Cultural Revolution (1966-1976)

-- Man walked on the moon (1969)

-- President Nixon's visit to China (1972)

-- USA and PRC renew diplomatic relations (1979)

-- China begins years of openness (1979-1999) and churches begin to bloom like wild flowers

-- Beijing Spring and Tiananmen Incident, June 4, 1989

-- British colony of Hong Kong reverts to PRC, July 1, 1997

-- Portuguese province reverts to PRC, Dec 31, 1999

Additional Reading on China
Religion, Christianity, History and Culture

Books

Adeney, David. *China: The Church's Long March.* Ventura, CA: Regal Books, 1985

Allen, Roland. *Missionary Methods: St. Paul's or Ours?* Chicago: Moody Press, 1959

Anderson, Courtney. *To the Golden Shore: The Life of Adoniram Judson.* Valley Forge: Judson Press, 1987

Anderson, Ken. *Bold as a Lamb.* Zondervan, 1991

Bao-Lord, Bette. *Legacies, A Chinese Mosaic*, N.Y.: Knopf, 1990

Barber, Noel. *The Fall of Shanghai.* London: Macmillan, 1979

Brown, G. Thompson, *Christianity in The People's Republic of China.* Atlanta: John Knox Press, 1983

Bryan, R.T. *Christianity's China Creations*, Richmond: Foreign Mission Board, 1927

Bull, Geoffrey T. *When Iron Gates Yield.* London: Hodder & Stoughton

Bull, Geoffrey T. God *Holds the Key.* London: Hodder & Stoughton, 1959

Burgess, Alan. *The Small Woman*, Re-print: Buccaneer Books, 1958

Cable and French. *George Hunter, Apostle of Turkestan.* London: China Inland Mission, 1948

Cauthen, Baker James, editor. *Advance: A History of Southern Baptist Foreign Missions.* Nashville: Broadman, 1970

Cauthen, Eloise Glass. *Higher Ground: Biography of Wiley B. Glass.* Nashville: Broadman Press, 1978

Chang Hsin-pao. *Commissioner Lin and the Opium War.* Cambridge: Harvard University Press, 1964

Cheng Nien. *Life and Death in Shanghai.* N.Y.: Grove Press, 1986

Chiu, Peter C.H. *An Historical Study of Nestorian Christianity in the Tang Dynasty,* Ph.D. Diss. Southwestern Baptist Theological Seminary, Fort Worth, Texas, 1987

Chu & Lind, editors. *A New Beginning.* Published by the Canada China Program of the Canadian Council of Churches, 1983

Clark, Carl A. *Who Walk in Faith, Saga of the Peter Lee Family,* private printing, Fort Worth, Texas, 1956

Cliff, Norman. *A Flame of Sacred Love, The Man Behind Hudson Taylor,* London: OM Publishers, 1998

Cliff, Norman. *Prisoners of the Samurai, Japanese Civilian Camps in China, 1941-1945.* London: Courtyard Publishers, 1998

Copeland, E. Luther. *The Southern Baptist Convention and the Judgment of History, The Taint of an Original Sin.:* University Press of America, 1995

Copeland, E. Luther. *World Mission Survival*. Nashville: Broadman, 1985

Covell, Ralph. *Mission Impossible: The Unreached Nosu on China's Frontier*. Pasadena, CA: Hope Publishing House, 1990

Covell, Ralph. *The Liberating Gospel in China*. Grand Rapids: Baker, 1995

Crawley, Winston. *Partners Across the Pacific, China and Southern Baptists: Into the Second Century*. Nashville: Broadman Press, 1986

Crawley, Winston. *New Frontiers in an Old World*. Nashville: Convention Press, 1962

Dawson, Raymond. *The Chinese Chameleon. An Analysis of European Conceptions of Chinese Civilization*. London: Oxford University Press, 1967

Dehoney, Wayne, *The Dragon and the Lamb*, Nashville: Broadman, 1986

Eddy, Sherwood, *Pathfinders of the World Missionary Crusade*, N.Y: Abington Press, 1969 reprint of 1945 book

Fielder, Maudie Albritton. *Life History: Maudie and John Wilson Fielder*. Unpublished memoirs. Southern Baptist Foreign Mission Board Archives. Richmond, Va.

Finn, James. *The Jews of China: Their Synagogue, Their Scriptures, Their History, &c.* Taipei, Taiwan (reprint): Ch'eng Wen Publishing Co., 1971

Fletcher, Jesse C. *Bill Wallace of China*. Nashville: Broadman Press, 1963

Heissig, Walther. *A Lost Civilization: The Mongols Rediscovered*. London: Thames and Hudson, 1966

Hersey, John. *The Call, An American missionary in China*. New York: Knopf. 1985 [a novel, but with unusual insight into the trials of 20th century China missions]

Houghton, Frank. *China Calling*, London: Inter-Varsity, 1936

Hughes, Richard. *Hong Kong Borrowed Place--Borrowed Time*. London: Andre Deutsch Ltd. 1968

Jen Yu-wen. *The Taiping Revolutionary Movement*. New Haven: Yale University Press, 1973 (a 600-page "summary" of Jen's multi-volume Chinese-language sets on the Taiping Movement.)

Kwong, Chunwah (Eric Kowng). *Hong Kong's Religions in Transition*. Waco, Texas, USA: The Tao Foundation, 2000.

Latourette, Kenneth Scott. *The Chinese, Their History and Culture*. 3rd edition, New York: Macmillan Co., 1945

Lautenschlager, Roy S. *On The Dragon Hills*. Philadelphia: Westminster Press, 1970

Lawrence, Carl. *The Church In China How It Survives and Prospers Under Communism*. Minneapolis: Bethany House Publishers, 1985

Liang Fa. *Quan Shi Liang Yan* (Good Words to Admonish the Age). Guangzhou and Malacca: Liang Fa Publisher, 1831.

Lin Yutang. *My Country and My People*. New York: The John Day Co., 1954

Lotz, Denton, editor. *Spring Has Returned--Listening to the Church in China*. McLean, Virginia: Baptist World Alliance, 1987

Lyall, Leslie. *Three of China's Mighty Men*. London: OMF Books, 1973

MacInnis, Donald. *Religious Policy and Practice in Communist China: A Documentary History*. N.Y.: Macmillan, 1972.

MacInnis, Donald. *Religion in China Today: Policy and Practice*. New York: Orbis Books, 1989

McCammon, Dorothy S. *We Tried to Stay*. Herald Press, 1953.

Memorials of Protestant Missionaries. Reprint, Ch'eng Wen Publishing Company, Taipei, Taiwan, 1967. Original edition published by the American Presbyterian Mission Press, Shanghai, 1867

Miao, Chester S., ed. *Christian Voices in China*. N.Y.: Friendship Press, 1948

Moffett, Samuel Hugh. *A History of Christianity in Asia, Vol. I, Beginnings to 1500*. San Francisco: Harpers, 1992

Mungello, David. *The Forgotten Christians of Hangzhou*. Honolulu: The University of Hawaii Press, 1994

Neill, Stephen. *Colonialism and Christian Missions*. New York: McGraw-Hill Book Co., 1966

Newbigin, Lesslie. *The Gospel in a Pluralist Society*. Grand Rapids: W. B. Eerdmans Publishing Company

Paton, David. *Christian Missions and the Judgment of God*. London: SCM Press Lt., 1953

239

Pollock, John. *A Foreign Devil in China*. Minn. World Wide Publishers, 1988

Pruitt, Ida. *A Daughter of Han: The Autobiography of a Chinese Working Woman*. Stanford: Stanford University Press (reprint, 1967)

Pruitt, Ida. *Old Madam Yin, A memoir of Peking Life*. Stanford: Stanford University Press, 1979

Records of the General Conference of the Protestant Missionaries of China, Shanghai, China, 1877. Reprinted by Ch'eng Wen Publishing Company, Taipei, Taiwan, 1973 (Original edition published by the Presbyterian Mission Press, Shanghai, China, 1978)

Sallee, Annie Jenkins. *Torchbearers in Honan*. 1948

Sallee, Annie Jenkins. *W. Eugene Salee, Christ's Ambassador*. 1933

Sowards, Genevieve and Erville, editors. *Burma Baptist Chronicle*. Rangoon: Board of Publications, Burma Baptist Convention, 1963

Smith, Carl T. *Chinese Christians: Elites, Middlemen, and the Church in Hong Kong*. Hong Kong: Oxford University Press, 1985

Spence, Jonathan D. Chinese *Roundabout*. New York: Norton, 1992

Spence, Jonathan D. *The Search for Modern China*. New York: W.W. Norton, 1990

Stamps, Elizabeth Belk. *To China With Love*, Ormand Beach, 1976

Still, Dorris Shelton, editor. *Chants From Shangri-La, Original Translation From the Tibetan by Flora Beal Shelton*. USA, 1939

Stockwell, F. Olin. *With God in Red China*, Harper & Bro., NY, 1953

Tang, Edmond & Jean-Paul Wiest, ed. *The Catholic Church in Modern China*, New York: Orbis Books, 1993

Taylor, Dr. and Mrs. Howard. *Hudson Taylor*, 2 volumes. London: China Inland Mission Press, 1958

Taylor, Hudson. *A Retrospect*. London: China Inland Press, 1954

Ting, K. H. *Chinese Christians Speak Out*. Beijing: New World Press, 1984

Towery, Britt. *The Penglai-Pingdu Baptist Memorials*. Hong Kong: Long Dragon Books, 1989

Towery, Britt. *Patterns,* (with Jody Towery) Hong Kong: Long Dragon Books, 1989

Towery, Britt. *Lao She, China's Master Storyteller*, Waco: Tao Foundation, 1999

Wardin, Albert, editor, *Baptists Around the World*. Nashville: Broadman and Holman Publishers, 1995 (China section by Towery, pp. 90-96)

Weatherspoon, J. B. *M. Theron Rankin*, Apostle of Advance. Nashville: Broadman Press, 1958

White, Theodore. *In Search of History*, Harper & Row, 1978

Whitehead, Raymond L. Editor, *No Longer Strangers, SelectedWritings of K. H. Ting.* New York: Orbis Books, 1989

Whyte, Bob. *Unfinished Encounter.* London: Collins, 1988

Wickeri, Philip. *Seeking the Common Ground.* New York: Orbis, 1988

Zhao Fusan. *Christianity in China.* Manila: De La Salle Univ. Press, 1986

Journals and Papers

Amity Press News Service, 13/F Ultraface Building, 5 Jordan Road, Kowloon, Hong Kong.<www.pacific.net.hk/~amityhk>

Bridge. Deng Zhaoming, editor. Tao Fong Shan Christian Center monthly, Kowloon, Hong Kong.

China Connections. Ms. Kathy Call, Executive Director, 458 South Pasadena Avenue, Pasadena, CA 91105

China Focus. Princeton China Initiative, Princeton N.J.

China News. General Assembly, Presbyterian Church, Atlanta.

China Study Project. Peter Leung, editor. English translations of China publications on religion. Inter-Church House, London

China Talk. Gail Colson, Editor. Hong Kong Liaison Office, United Methodist Church

Chinese Around the World. Published monthly in Chinese and English: Hong Kong/Singapore

Chinese Theological Review. 1985-1995 editions. Janice Wickeri, editor. Translations of Chinese sermons, theological essays and related material.

Commission Magazine. The missionary journal of the Southern Baptist Foreign Mission Board, Richmond, Va. (September, 1967, on "Red Guards" and Oct./Nov., 1987, Insights into the SBC FMB's (now IMB) CSI organization)

Journal of Church and State, Vol. 32, Number 3, Summer, 1990. Waco: J.M. Dawson Institute of Church-State Studies. Baylor University, "Interview with K. H. Ting" by Towery, pp. 719-724.

Journal of Oriental Studies, Vol. XII, Numbers 1 and 2, Hong Kong University Press, 1974

King, Majorie. "A Georgia Evangelist in the Celestial empire: Cicero Washington Pruitt (1857-1946) and the Southern Baptist Mission in Shantung," in *Georgia's East Asian Connection: Into the Twenty-First Century*

Lawton, W.W. Unpublished letters of W.W. Lawton, 1898-1899. SBC Copies in the Texas Collection, Baylor University, Waco, Texas

Realm of Reality. Occasional journal written and edited by Britt Towery in Taiwan and Hong Kong, 1958-1990

Tian Feng. Shen Cheng'en, editor. Monthly Chinese-language publication of the China Christian Council, 169 Yuanmingyuan, Shanghai, People's Republic of China

ABOUT THE AUTHOR

Britt Towery has spent over thirty years in Chinese ministry in Taiwan, Hong Kong and Mainland China. He and his wife Jody are Howard Payne University, Brownwood, Texas, graduates and began the First Baptist Church of San Manuel, Arizona and the Pingtung Baptist Church in Southern Taiwan. He built bridges of understanding and ministry between many of the Southern Baptist Convention's International Mission Board personnel and the China Christian Council. He placed many English teachers and medical technicians in China universities from 1982-1992. He is the former director of the Asian Studies Program, Baylor University in Waco, Texas, and the founder and director of the Tao Foundation, a channel for sharing needs and truths from the East to the West.

Printed in the United States
24117LVS00001B/82-93

9 781587 214103